NAKED
— AND —
UNASHAMED

**The Journey Toward Sexual Fulfillment
in Christian Marriage**

DR. STACY L. SPENCER

STASIS
PRODUCTIONS

NAKED AND UNASHAMED

The Journey Toward Sexual Fulfillment in Christian Marriage

Scripture quotations marked KJV are taken from the Holy Bible, *King James Version*. Scripture quotations marked NIV are taken from the Holy Bible, *New International Version*. Copyright © 1973, 1978, 1984 by International Bible Society, used by permission of Zondervan Publishing House. Scripture quotations marked NKJV are taken from the *New King James Version*. Copyright © 1979, 1980, 1982 by Thomas Nelson, Inc. Used by Permission. Scripture quotations marked MSG are taken from *The Message*. Copyright © 1993, 1994, 1995, 1996, 2000, 2001, 2002. Used by permission of NavPress Publishing Group. Scripture quotations marked NRSV are taken from *New Revised Standard Version Bible*. Copyright © 1989, Division of Christian Education of the National Council of the Churches of Christ in the United States of America. Used by permission. All rights reserved. Scripture quotations marked ESV are from *the Holy Bible, English Standard Version*. Copyright © 2001 by Crossway Bibles, a division of Good News Publishers. Used by permission. All rights reserved.

Printed in the United States of America.

ISBN: 978-0-9819710-1-8
     978-0-9819710-0-1

Anatomical Illustrations by Glenda Warren Yancey

To Order Additional Copies, Contact:
    Lori McGee
    3581 Hickory Hill Road
    Memphis, TN 38115
    mcgee.lori@stacyspencer.org
    (901) 433-3871/office • (901) 433-3872/fax

DISCLAIMER

Naked and Unashamed is intended to provide biblically-based education and general information to consensual pre-marital and married adults. Laws vary from state to state, and are subject to change. However, the author has taken all meaningful and reasonable precautions to ensure the accuracy of the material presented in this book.

Neither the author nor the publisher assume any liability resulting from the use or application of information in this book. Parents are advised to take special care to keep this book out of the reach of minor children.

DEDICATION

I dedicate this book to my lovely wife, Rhonda. She has been the wind beneath my wings and the inspiration behind this book. When I first met her in college, I knew in the spirit she was my "help mate, bone of my bone and flesh of my flesh." But it took me years of maturity to be able to appreciate the totality of who she is as a gift from God. I am blessed to have such a special woman in my life who makes me a better man.

I also thank the wonderful members of New Direction Christian Church in Memphis, Tennessee, where I pastor one of the most amazingly radical churches in the world. They are a great group of believers who challenge me every week to stay real, relevant, and sometimes raw with the truth of Jesus Christ.

I thank God for all of my family and friends who have continuously encouraged me to birth this book. Through my labor, may God be glorified and His married children edified.

ACKNOWLEDGMENTS

When I look back over my life there are so many mentors along and influences upon my journey. My teachers ranged from old farmers and hunters in the country to professors and pastors in the nation's urban areas. God has allowed my path to cross with many impacting people who have left indelible marks upon the hallway of my heart.

I must acknowledge my pastor in my hometown of Olmstead, Kentucky, Rev. Quinton Yates, who preached me into ministry with a sermon entitled, "Untie Yourself So the Lord Can Use You." He told me, "Son, whether it's at your house or Morehouse, study to show yourself approved." I have great appreciation for Rev. Chris Battle, then-pastor of State Street Baptist Church in Bowling Green, Kentucky, who told me, "If you are going to preach you need to go to seminary. Don't be in nobody's pulpit talking ignorance." Also, thank God for Dr. Kevin W. Cosby, pastor of St. Stephen Baptist Church in Louisville, Kentucky, who awakened me to being a Christian who is socially conscious, culturally relevant, and "out of the box."

It was Dr. Alvin O'Neal Jackson, then-pastor of Mississippi Boulevard Christian Church in Memphis, Tennessee, who helped to bridge my calling to my destiny. He showed me how to have a shepherd's heart in a mega-church. Dr. Frank Anthony Thomas showed me how to walk with integrity and intelligence, and to weather storms with dignity.

I thank God for my first hero, my mama, Carolyn Spencer, who raised three kids by herself, survived breast cancer, and got her R.N. degree at the same time. Mother, you are a strong woman. I'd like to thank my dad, Rev. Sammy Spencer, for accepting his call into the ministry when I was just a teenager and breaking the curse in our family of boys being raised without their fathers. I love you, Dad.

To my brother and sister, I appreciate all the love and support through the years. You were my first congregation in the wilderness. Having to grow up fast and help raise you both taught me a lot. I love you and I am so proud to see you blossom into the adults that you are today.

I appreciate my loving aunts, Marilyn and Janet, who bought me clothes and gave me shelter. I'm grateful to Uncle Sylvester "Babe" Cage for teaching me to hunt and to work. Thank God for all the salt-of-the-earth country folks who grounded me in life to survive the matrix of big city façades.

Thank God for real friends like Pastor Monte Campbell—who always finds a way to speak a prophetic word in my life when I need it most. To all of my staff, armor bearers, and members at New Direction Christian Church—thank you for praying and supporting your pastor.

Thanks to Dr. Kevin W. Cosby for believing in the need for this book and to Rev. Olivia M. Cloud for editing this detailed book that I wrestled from my mind, body, and spirit. Finding a good editor is like finding a good barber; I don't trust everybody with my head and my heart. Thank you, Olivia, for helping me to flush out my honest thoughts and for making me wrestle with relevancy and what is really needed for married couples to stay married and for the church to speak truth to life.

Thank You, God, for not giving up on me, and for allowing my pain, my mistakes, and my learning to be blessings to other young couples who, hopefully, will avoid the pitfalls that the enemy has set and silence has perpetrated.

Bless you all as you go back into the garden where God's children can live *Naked and Unashamed.*

CONTENTS

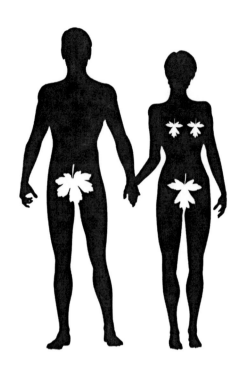

And Adam said:
"This is now bone of my bones
And flesh of my flesh;
She shall be called Woman,
Because she was taken out of Man."
Therefore a man shall leave his father
and mother and be joined to his wife,
and they shall become one flesh.
And they were both naked, the man
and his wife, and were not ashamed.
                            Genesis 2:23-25 (NKJV)

INTRODUCTION
The Secret Garden

"The Secret Garden," a song written and produced by Quincy Jones in the early 1990s, is an amalgamation of great R&B love song artists, including Barry White, Al B. Sure!, James Ingram, and El Debarge. Their melodious voices croon with great eloquence and vivid allure that serenade the listener on a journey back to the place where Adam and Eve smelled the sweet sensation of wild flowers, luscious fruit, running water, and plush grass. Much like the original garden must have been for Adam and Eve, Jones's love song is a description of an emotional and physical place of sensuality and intimacy that is not commonplace in relationships.

The elusive Garden of Eden (see Genesis 2:24-25) has always seemed to be a place of intrigue and passion—seemingly sacred and forbidden. But the Bible describes the garden as a place of purity and innocence, a place where God invited His creation to come and enjoy its benefits.

The human prototypes Adam and Eve were introduced to one another in the garden. In Genesis, God noticed the loneliness of Adam, whom God made responsible for the care of the garden and gave dominion over all the created things.

But as God has already determined, there is something incomplete about a man who doesn't have his "help mate." As James Brown sang, "It's a man's world, but it wouldn't be nothing without a woman…."

When God put Adam to sleep, He pulled out of him a woman. When Adam awakened, he saw Eve and immediately felt a close connection with her, calling her "bone of my bones and flesh of my flesh" (Genesis 2:23, NIV). Then, as the Bible describes the Creation story, the most powerful verse of this story is when it is stated in the book of Genesis that they were naked and unashamed (see Genesis 2:25).

Naked and Unashamed

Their blissful state of being would not last. Adam and Eve disobeyed God, resulting in their banishment from this beautiful sanctuary.

> When the woman saw that the fruit of the tree was good for food and pleasing to the eye, and also desirable for gaining wisdom, she took some and ate it. She also gave some to her husband, who was with her, and he ate it. Then the eyes of both of them were opened, and they realized they were naked; so they sewed fig leaves together and made coverings for themselves. Then the man and his wife heard the sound of the LORD God as he was walking in the garden in the cool of the day, and they hid from the LORD God among the trees of the garden. But the LORD God called to the man, "Where are you?" He answered, "I heard you in the garden, and I was afraid because I was naked; so I hid." And he said, "Who told you that you were naked? Have you eaten from the tree that I commanded you not to eat from?" (Genesis 3:6-11, NIV).

Before Adam and Eve disobeyed God and were cast out of the garden, their sexuality was in a place of wholeness. Sexual wholeness is established when a man and woman are compatible, not just compromising in their physical relationship. A marital partner is compromised when he or she makes personality adjustments to fit his or her spouse's preference.

Adam and Eve's nakedness in the Garden (see verse 25) suggests that they were at ease with one another without any fear of exploitation or potential for evil. Such fellowship was shattered later via the Fall and only a measure is retained in marriage when a couple begins to feel at ease with each other. Adam and Eve's nakedness, though literal, also suggests sinlessness. They were in such a state of innocence that they were not even conscious of their nakedness. It was only after the Fall that they attempted to hide their nakedness.

"Who told you, that you were naked?" God asked Adam a good question, one that many men and women need to ask themselves. Toddlers can run around in their birthday suits without much fuss, but somewhere around three years of age they are conditioned to become keenly aware of their nakedness. Is it because concerned parents educated them, or does something innate guide them to cover up? In any case, we learn early in life that nakedness is something to be ashamed of. Our shame toward our nakedness is also cultural.

Many of South Africa's early travelers and missionaries regarded the Bushmen they encountered as utterly distasteful—one of the reasons being their nakedness. The Reverend James Read, a British missionary, in a letter dated August 5, 1840, appealed to his friends back at home to send clothes for the "poor naked Bushmen." No one had told the Bushmen that it was bad to be naked; therefore, they harbored no shame regarding their condition.

Perhaps the more relevant question for couples today is: "Who told you that being naked is shameful?" That question is important whether the nakedness is physical or emotional. "Who told you that you and your husband had to make love with the lights off? Who told you that it is wrong to enjoy seeing each other naked? Who told you that enjoying your own nakedness was shameful? Who told you that you were naked?"

Overcoming old ideas that hinder sexual fulfillment in marriage requires the cooperation of each spouse. The husband and the wife must be committed to taking the steps necessary to unveiling themselves and live with each other naked and unashamed, just like Adam and Eve before the Fall.

Before the Fall, God made provisions for the first man and woman in the environment He had created and allowed them to inhabit. God established the rules for living in the Garden and told Adam and Eve they could eat from any tree—except the forbidden tree. It was God's compromise. God had given them plenty of latitude, but was firm in the one area where they didn't need any more room. Eve, and subsequently Adam, tested God to see how far they could take the compromise by eating from the forbidden tree. Subsequently, Adam and Eve damaged their relationship with God and with each other by attempting to stretch the compromise.

When they were living under a healthy divine compromise, they were naked and unashamed, eating from any tree except one. They compromised further with the wrong one—the serpent, the deceiver—and moved to being naked and ashamed.

A husband or wife compromises with the wrong one when he or she shifts attention to a third party—someone or something outside of the marriage covenant. Just as he manifested himself as a serpent in the creation narrative, the devil can manifest himself in whatever form he needs to engage anyone in an unhealthy compromise. He can become the understanding, listening ear that a wife doesn't get at home. He may be the attentive personality who notices a married woman's new fragrance and compliments her on it. He may be the hot body that a husband and father had at home before the kids were born. He may make a man or woman feel young and sexually desirable again, arousing feelings thought to be long dead.

This spirit of deception seeks and often finds a crack of vulnerability in either the husband or the wife, or even both. What begins as a small crack can grow into a chasm that leaves a wide gap for conversations that should only be had between a husband and wife. Once the gulf has opened to sufficiently separate the couple, unhealthy compromise finds its way in.

Unhealthy compromise with a deceptive third party breeds unholy alliances and devastating decisions. Compromises like affairs (whether physical, Internet, or emotional), pornography, swinging, and *menage-a-trois* (threesomes) are made when spouses allow themselves to be vulnerable with Satan and his seductive influences.

Every relationship requires compromises, but these should be adjustments rather than overhauls. When a person begins to make major or self-deprecating compromises or feels the need to do a complete personality makeover in order to sustain a relationship, there may be a compatibility problem. The capacity to truly love one's spouse approximates agape—unconditional love. Possessing this type of love entails taking inventory of a spouse's flaws and being willing to accept him or her as is. As Bishop Noel Jones has stated, "You are not going to find anybody without flaws." Therefore, it is best to be realistic and fair in assessing one's spouse. A person's capacity to love must be rooted in agape—the unconditional, unfailing love received by all those who are in Christ. It is the kind of love that compelled God to give the world His only begotten Son (see John 3:16).

During a women's conference in Little Rock, Arkansas, I heard Bishop Jones say that in order for a relationship to be whole, the people involved must be compatible. When a person continues to compromise in relationships, he or she is reduced to fitting in by becoming something artificial. When two people are compatible it is because they each have the capacity to love the other for who that person is. Never-ending compromise is a sign of incompatibility.

From the outset of the marriage, the husband and wife should have already established the compromises they know to be true between them and God. When spouses have the capacity to love each other as is sexually, they achieve sexual wholeness. When a woman who has been trained to say "no" is able to listen to the man who has been trained not to hear "no," they can achieve sexual wholeness because they have begun to communicate.

Bishop Jones also shared how society teaches girls to say "no" to sex (to preserve their purity) while simultaneously teaching boys (by saying nothing) that they should not accept "no." By the time these two get married there is a power struggle between them. In the wife's subconscious mind, giving in to a man's desires—even though he is her husband—marks her as being loose or immoral. In the husband's mind, her refusal is an indication of her lack of love and desire for him. Both the husband and wife fail to take into account what the other was taught to believe about sex. They enter the relationship broken, covering themselves and failing to achieve the kind of openness that is needed to live naked and unashamed. A great number of couples live in this state of brokenness for years, many of them eventually dissolving their marriage.

Sexual wholeness is modern-day Adam and Eve living together in bliss, naked and unashamed, because they have learned how to say "yes" to each other and "no" to the devil. Being sexually whole (for married couples) means being like Adam and Eve before the Fall—naked and unashamed. They had no need for clothes or cover-ups.

A great deal of meaning and wisdom is packed into the phrase "naked and unashamed." Some couples do know the feeling from the early months and years of their marriage. But they have lost it and do not know how to retrieve the excitement, the curiosity, and the desire they once had for each other. How do married couples get back to that elusive place where they can relate to each other without barriers, restrictions, or hindrances and live naked and unashamed?

The plain truth is that Christian married couples do not seem to be any more capable of getting to that place than non-Christian couples. They do not know how to get to the place where they are naked and know no shame, and few leaders seem equipped or willing to help them get there. Today, Christendom seems replete with sexual scandals—from Jimmy Swaggart to Ted Haggard. Married Christians, even those in leadership, seem as inept as the rest of the world at maintaining stable, godly marital relationships. Rumors of infidelity and divorce and reports of domestic abuse are rampant among clergy, but rare are the post-modern prototypes of Christian couples living naked and unashamed.

As churches attempt to dissuade congregants from divorce, recent research confirms George Barna's findings from a decade ago that born-again Christians have the same likelihood of divorce as non-Christians. Among married, born-again Christians, 35 percent have experienced a divorce. That figure is identical to the outcome among married adults who are not born again.[1]

Barna noted that one reason for the parallel divorce statistics is because non-born-again adults cohabitate at a much higher rate, effectively side-stepping marriage—and divorce. Among born-again adults, 80 percent have been married, compared to just 69 percent among the non-born-again segment. If the non-born-again population were to marry at the same rate as the born-again group, it is likely that their divorce statistic would be roughly 38 percent—only marginally higher than that of the born-again group, but still surprisingly close.

Life Outside the Garden

When couples live outside the garden, there is a constant tug-of-war between husband and wife as to who will get his or her way. Both husband and wife are starved for the sex and the affection they crave. Their marriage is a union of constant arguments and disharmony because of their inability to connect at the core level of intimacy. Eventually, this sexual disharmony can lead to deception, as it did with Eve and the serpent. Marriages lacking sexual harmony also can lead to sexually addictive behavior, usually exercised in a deceptive fashion. When the eroticism is not fully embraced within marriage, the couple's unfulfilled desires can cause them to split off and be exiled from the Garden. Usually they split in search of self-gratification that can only serve to weaken the marital bond.

In his book, *Internet Pornography: A Shadow in the Church*, author Dr. Theodore L. Baldick, profoundly illustrates the fall of Adam and Eve from the Garden. He writes that the breakdown begins when doubt enters into the relationship between Adam (husband) and Eve (wife). The deceiver begins infecting one of the spouses with doubt: "Did God really say...?" Once the seeds of doubt are firmly planted, curiosity drives that spouse to look outside the covenant with God, ignoring the fact that God has given everything they need.

Next, the deceiver hits them with deprivation, "He is keeping you from...." One spouse begins to believe, "I'm missing out on something." His or her curiosity is further aroused, which leads to thoughts that point away from the other spouse, away from the Garden, and, worst of all, away from God.

Then comes desire. Feelings of deprivation give rise to desire. Either spouse begins to long for what he or she feels is missing from the marriage. This temptation, when nurtured by doubt, deprivation, and desire, escalates into craving—a hunger to see and experience what is being missed.

Then comes the decision to take action. Eve "took some [of the forbidden fruit] and ate." A decision may take only a few seconds or it may have been calculated over for days, weeks, months—even years.

Walter [all names in these scenarios have been changed] is a minister who had reached the point of deciding to look outside of his marriage for fulfillment. He met a young lady while out with a mutual friend and was immediately attracted to her. A few days later, he called the woman on the phone and invited her to dinner. Despite his protestations of discretion, she was firm in her disinterest in dating a married man. He decided to give the pursuit one last try and sent her a dozen roses, along with an open invitation to dinner. All the woman could do was wonder, "Why doesn't he spend that kind of energy on his wife? When's the last time he sent her flowers?" Walter had made a decision to step outside and taste the forbidden fruit and had embarked on a journey to find it.

After decision comes desperation: "They saw they were naked and were ashamed." They seek to cover up what God has provided for them. They can no longer be open with each other. The transparency and openness is gone and the games, lies, and deceptions begin.

The last state is despair: "They hid from God." The response to feelings of despair is to isolate oneself from others and, ultimately, from God. A man who is in despair feels a sense of helplessness; he becomes irritable toward his wife. The two cannot get back to a place of agreement and there is an imbalance in their sexuality. The husband begins to blame the wife for his strong sex drive because he decided to eat from the forbidden tree. He blames the woman for his decision.

Pornography is just one example of the kind of detrimental elements that couples bring into their relationship if they do not learn to find wholeness in their own marriage bed. Their despair does not have to exist if both can learn to channel their desire toward each other rather than looking to the "forbidden tree." Often the forbidden tree is sought because of miscommunication, rather than the sex itself. But two people who are sexually compatible can learn to communicate about what is acceptable and not acceptable. When couples live outside the Garden they are not talking—or doing anything else for that matter. They are blaming one another—and the cycle of doubt, deprivation, desire, decision, desperation, and despair continues.

Getting Back to the Garden

The Garden of Eden mentioned in the book of Genesis had two angels guarding the entrance with flaming swords so that Adam and Eve could not return after the Fall. Something is still blocking re-entry today—and there should be re-entry after the work that Jesus did on the Cross. Married couples should be able to re-enter the Garden and live together naked and unashamed.

Throughout the book, we will explore ways that couples can live naked and unashamed from a biblical context. "Naked," for the purpose of this book, is a state where husbands and wives no longer hide from themselves sexually, being comfortable in their own skin. "Naked" is being able to embrace one's sexuality without the pollution of corrupt sexual views.

Our sexual views become corrupted when society has infiltrated our understanding regarding what is acceptable and unacceptable. For example, swinging is making a popular resurgence, despite the prevalence of sexually transmitted diseases. Couples are entertaining the idea of exchanging partners, some with the misguided notion that swinging will save their marriage. Additionally, same-sex marriage is gaining acceptance as an alternative to biblical marriage. Sexual promiscuity is central to much of the "entertainment" on television, even as rates of HIV and teen pregnancy cases are on the rise.

Pornography has become a replacement for intimacy in many marriages as husbands emotionally disconnect from their wives in search of immediate, albeit false intimacy with their printed or electronic lovers. Divorce rates are staggering as Christian couples who decide they are just not happy gather at the well of divorce court, searching for water and facing up to the fact that "this fifth husband is not yours either" (see John 4:18).

"Unashamed," as defined for the purposes of this book, means being free from guilt because of past actions or fear of future actions fueled by condemning thoughts that have been passed down. "Unashamed" means reaching a healthy biblical understanding regarding what is acceptable before God for a husband and wife to enjoy in their bedroom and it not be defiled.

When couples learn how to get back in the Garden there is a sigh of relief between husband and wife because they are in the place where they belong. The wife is getting the affection and satisfaction she deserves. And because the wife is getting the affection she deserves, the husband is getting the sex he wants. Both are connecting on a level that fills their emotional tanks and keeps them in a sense of perpetual paradise.

On an episode of Oprah's television show, Dr. Mehmet Oz had a quiz that asked how often married couples in a healthy relationship should have sex: a) once a week; b) twice a month; c) twelve times a year; or d) two hundred times a year. The answer was over two hundred times a year. He said the frequency of a couple's sexual activity is a way to monitor each spouse's physical health. If a man is able to have sex with his wife over two hundred times a year, which averages to about 3.5 times a week, then his blood flow is good because he is able to have an erection.

Dr. Oz also said that sex is a spiritual connection. When a person has sex with someone he or she deeply loves, it creates a spiritual connection. Dr. Oz is on to something. When spouses acquire the balance of sexual wholeness in the Garden, there is a connection that gets couples close to one another and close to God. There is a closeness that does not allow the deceiver to enter their relationship. The adulteress cannot break up a happy home when the man is satisfied. The charming male co-worker can't swoon away a wife with sappy kudos because she is already getting them from her husband. Great sex is a way that couples stay connected and keep the devil out!

My hope in writing this book is to help married couples, post-modern Adam and Eve, get back into that secret Garden where they can live and relate to one another, naked and unashamed. All couples are invited to come into God's Garden—where passion runs deep between a husband and wife—and be naked and unashamed.

*"We need to be talking
about sex.
The school does and people
on the street do
and TV does, but Christians don't.
Address the issue!
Just don't tell me to act like
I don't feel these things."*

CHAPTER ONE
The Theology of Sex

Dr. Phil
"When sex is good its 10% of the marriage When its bad its 90% of the marriage."
The world took sex out of context. Its a god thing.

Thought: Marriage was going to be the panacea

This sentiment was expressed by a pastor who recognizes the schizophrenia within the Christian community regarding sex. In the book of Genesis, God commands humanity to be fruitful and multiply. The only way human beings can multiply is through sexual activity, but the majority of the Christian community treats sex as a necessary evil rather than a gift from God. Describing the attitude in the homes where they were raised, 76 percent of Christians surveyed reported that sex was never discussed.

Christians have a lot of shame about sex and the natural, God-given sexual urges human beings have. Some are even more ashamed that they like those urges and feelings. Sex is a real and natural part of Christian living, but we do not talk about it. We do not teach our children about it, nor do we counsel engaged couples about what to expect in the marriage bed. Instead, we simply encourage people to marry so they will not be found guilty of fornication.

It is then assumed that, having obtained a permissible sex partner (i.e., a spouse), a person will have no more struggles with lust and sin. Nothing could be further from the truth. Marriage does not remedy lust. If anything, it complicates the problem by introducing a new set of difficulties.

The state of Tennessee is often regarded as the "buckle" of the Bible Belt, being home to a number of religious organizations and boasting a large number of evangelical Christians. However, Tennessee also has one of the highest per capita divorce rates in the nation. One sociologist speculated that the reason for the high divorce rate among believers who profess not to believe in divorce is that evangelical Christians may marry more quickly in order to legitimize sexual activity. In their haste to avoid fornication, they may overlook other important characteristics in finding a spouse. Marriage in and of itself can be a poor mechanism for controlling lust because a bad marriage will only yield even more thoughts of lust for someone outside the marriage. Marriage will not eliminate feelings of lust.

Minister/author Frederick Buechner articulated this Christian dilemma when he wrote: "Lust is the ape that gibbers in our loins. Tame him as we will by day, he rages all the wilder in our dreams by night. Just when we think we're safe from him, he raises up his ugly head and smirks, and there's no river in the world flows cold and strong enough to strike him down. Almighty God, why dost thou deck men out with such a loathsome toy?"

So why do human beings have the ability to lust when all we are ever told is that it is bad and that we should get rid of it if it ever pops up?

The Christian sexual struggle includes finding a place for lust to dwell. Many believers desire to be free of the tormentor—lust. They hopelessly long for the seeming one-dimensional life of the Puritans of early American culture.

When most people think of the Puritans, they think of a bunch of fairly drab religious people who hated any type of amusement or frivolity, especially sex. While the Puritan lifestyle pales in comparison to the "anything goes," sexually-charged culture of today, a close look at the Puritan view of sex reveals a surprising discovery—they were having "sex in the city" as well.

For a long time, people in church have believed that Puritans disdained sex and shunned any kind of enjoyment as it pertained to sexuality. Interestingly enough, H.L. Mencken remarked facetiously, "A Puritan is someone who is deathly afraid that someone, somewhere, is having fun."

The truth is, Puritans had no particular issue with sex. They knew that both men and women are subject to sexual desires. They certainly knew that women experience arousal and orgasms. In fact, the conventional Protestant wisdom of the sixteenth and seventeenth centuries was that women might grow ill or mad if they do not experience regular sexual release. Puritans believed that sex is reserved for the marriage bed and that adultery and premarital sex are sins. They also believed that married couples should embark upon lovemaking prayerfully, remembering that sexual pleasure is a gift from God. Their beliefs regarding sex were in perfect agreement with Anglicans and other Protestants of the same period, and with quite a few modern-day Christians as well.

The Puritan doctrine of sex was a turning point in the cultural history of the West. The Puritans devalued celibacy, glorified "equally yoked" marriage, affirmed married sex as both necessary and pure, established the ideal of wedded romantic love, and exalted the role of the wife. This complex of ideals and values achieved its most eloquent and beautiful expression in John Milton's picture of the married life of Adam and Eve in his epic literary work, *Paradise Lost*. In portraying the perfect marriage in *Book Four*, Milton went out of his way to show that Adam and Eve enjoyed sexual union before the Fall. In *Book Four*, Milton highlights the usual Puritan themes: the biblical basis for affirming sex (as evidenced by several key biblical illusions in the passage); the differentiation between animal lust and human sexual love; understanding sexual fulfillment within a domestic context; and general romantic overtones of the passage.

The early Puritans embraced their sexuality through their faith, yet for many decades sexuality has been deemed taboo in the church. It is one of those things that everybody is doing but is too holy to speak on. The Christian church has long held a simple and succinct view toward sex: "Just don't do it; and for heaven's sake don't talk about it!" The church has used shame and guilt to hold control over the reins of lust.

It is good to encourage and support people to wait until marriage before engaging in sexual activity. The problem is that when people get married, neither spouse knows what to do with the feelings of shame and guilt they have held toward sex for most of their lives. Thus, they bring shame and guilt into the bedroom and rob each other of the intimacy that marriage is supposed to bring.

My wife and I conducted a "40 Nights of Great Sex" workshop for over 250 married couples. We initiated this workshop because we had encountered too many married couples in church lacking sexual fulfillment. As a result, many of them were having problems. As Dr. Phil has noted, "When sex is good, it's 10 percent of a marriage. When it's bad, it's 90 percent of a marriage."

During the course of the workshop, it was somewhat surprising to discover that the majority of couples there had never discussed sex with their parents. The subject had been considered taboo. The couples who attended ranged from having been married six months to over fifty years. Out of the entire group, only two spouses acknowledged having conversations with their parents about sex!

Many Christians enter into marriage believing that sex is not something to be discussed openly. As a result, many marriages suffer from layers of cover-up that make it hard for husband and wife to have honest communication because they are not naked and, therefore, not easily known. Instead, they engage in layers of unproductive conversations because one spouse refuses to disclose his or her true self. There has been a break in their understanding of who God created them to be. They have refused to turn back to God and now they are in hiding.

When either spouse breaks from God it will cause the couple to lose their connection with each other. Spouses are supposed to be in a state of nakedness—transparency—but instead, marriages are suffocating from too many layers that block communication and allow people to hide from real intimacy. When couples understand that God created humanity as sexual beings, they can discover that their sexual intimacy is made stronger through spiritual intimacy with God.

Who Told You that You Were Naked?

Holman Bible Dictionary defines "naked" as being without clothes (see Genesis 2:25; Job 1:21; Ecclesiastes 5:15; Amos 2:16; Micah 1:8) or poorly clothed (see Deuteronomy 28:48; Matthew 25:36-44; James 2:15). However, the phrase "to uncover the nakedness of" means to have sexual intercourse (see Leviticus 18:6-19; 20:11, 17-21).

In the Bible, nakedness frequently occurs in conjunction with shame (see Genesis 3:7; 9:21-27; Isaiah 47:3; Ezekiel 16:8, 36-37). It is this latter definition that has been associated with nakedness in the church. We have been naked and ashamed because of our traditional, albeit misguided, notions about nakedness.

I remember being uncomfortable with my nakedness as an insecure teenager. For some reason I was a late bloomer. I could not grow body hair. I weighed ninety pounds, and was 4'11" in the eleventh grade. I played football, trying to keep up with the "big boys." After practice, the other guys would walk around naked, popping each other with towels as they headed for the showers. I would make a beeline for the back door, fully clothed in dirty, sour shoulder pads, trying to avoid the embarrassment of being naked. My mother, knowing my insecurity, would just roll the window down because she knew her young son was too ashamed to get naked among his peers.

How many Christian couples are riding out sour marriages because they have not learned how to get past their insecurities and be comfortable with their nakedness? The Sexual Revolution of the 1960s never caught up with the people in the church because Christians are uncomfortable with being naked.

For the longest, Christians have been making beelines for the light switch in their bedroom so they can stay in the dark and hide their nakedness during intercourse. They have not acclimated themselves to the many pleasure points of the human anatomy because their nakedness has been associated with shame. In the book, *What Your Mother Never Told You about Sex*, author Hilda Hutcherson, M.D. begins with recollections of her first sexual encounter: "It was billed as the greatest day of my life by the man who was to be my husband. He touched me slowly and gently. Softly. Lovingly. And as his hand brushed my breasts, my mother's "bad-girl" face appeared out of nowhere."

"Good girls don't."

"Don't let boys touch you."

"Keep your skirt down and your panties up."

"His hands touched my essence. Warm breath and moist kisses covered me. And as he neared my intact hymen, my preacher's "Thou shalt not" face materialized."

"Fire and brimstone."

"Hell and damnation."

"Sin, sin, sin."

Many couples take these images into their bedroom with them and can't enjoy their nakedness because of their preconceived, misguided notions about their nakedness. There is a new sexual revolution, as taught by Ed Young on his Web site (www.edyoung.com). Young shares how there is so much more to explore in the "big bed" of marriage and encourages couples not to settle for the "little bed" of sexual dysfunctions. Young asserts that the church has not dealt with a balanced sexuality; therefore, Christians are ashamed of their nakedness and their sexuality.

While on a journey to a remote part of South Africa, we encountered a young lady breastfeeding in public. A couple of the men in our group were surprised to see a young woman breastfeeding in public without covering her breast. One of our guides explained that the sight of a woman's exposed breast does not sexually arouse African men because it is culturally acceptable. It was not until Christian missionaries came to different parts of Africa and told the natives they were naked that covering up became an issue. Who told you that you were naked?

Shame regarding the human body is not inborn—it is learned. Many of South Africa's early travelers and missionaries regarded the Bushmen they encountered as utterly distasteful, only one of the reasons being because of their nakedness. The Reverend James Read, in a letter dated August 5, 1840, appealed to his friends in Britain to send clothes for the "poor naked Bushmen."

The Hebrew word translated naked essentially means "easily able to be known in view of the fact that nothing is hidden." After Creation, the husband and a wife were naked and easily knew each other. Their nakedness as described in Genesis 2:25 suggests that they were at ease with one another without fear of exploitation or potential for evil. This fellowship was shattered after the Fall, however, and only a small measure of this perfect state is attained in marriage after a couple begins to feel at ease with each other. In the book of Genesis, Adam and Eve's nakedness, though literal, also suggests sinlessness. They were in a state of innocence and were not even conscious of their nakedness. Only after the Fall did they try to hide their nakedness.

Christians traditionally have focused on the shame associated with nakedness and have not focused on the original blessedness of nakedness. Adam and Eve were naked and without shame. As Christians, we need to study the Scripture passages that address the sanctity of being naked. There is joy in being naked and unashamed with your spouse. It is actually in the Bible! God wants husbands and wives to be naked in the "big bed" with each other, and this is confirmed in His Word.

Let's look at some of these scriptures and "turn on the light" to reveal the blessedness of nakedness.

1. Sex is not dirty.

> Drink water from your own cistern,
> running water from your own well.
> Should your springs overflow in the streets,
> your streams of water in the public squares?
> Let them be yours alone,
> never to be shared with strangers.
> May your fountain be blessed,

> and may you rejoice in the wife of your youth.
> A loving doe, a graceful deer—
> may her breasts satisfy you always,
> may you ever be captivated by her love.
>
> (Proverbs 5:15-19, NIV)

The writer of Proverbs 5:15-19 was admonishing young husbands to fully enjoy their wives. He asked, "Why waste your streams (sexual energy) in the streets when they belong to your spouse only?" The writer told husbands to "enjoy the wife of your youth" and is explicit about enjoying her breasts. The writer spoke of one wife even though polygamy was accepted during the time the Old Testament was written. This could be an early reference to the practice of monogamy, to be introduced later in the Christian tradition; or, it also could be confirmation that God intended for husbands to have only one wife.

The writer was encouraging young men to be faithful and fulfill their sexual desires with their wives only. What great advice for young married couples today! A man is to enjoy his wife's breasts; and a wife should enjoy her husband's stream. There is no need for spouses to go outside the marriage bed and waste their sexuality with strangers when everything they need is at home. To take it even further, the word cistern, found in the book of Proverbs passage, also can be understood as the woman's vagina. A look at the definition of cistern reveals one of its meanings as "a fluid-containing sac or cavity in an organism." Therefore, a husband ought to quench his sexual thirst at his own cistern.

2. The marriage bed is to remain undefiled.

Hebrews 13:4 (NKJV) reads: "Marriage is honorable among all, and the bed undefiled; but fornicators and adulterers God will judge." When a man and woman are married, what they do in their bedroom is between them and God. Scripture passages like Leviticus 18 tell us what is acceptable and not acceptable, but the most important factor is that the husband and wife are in agreement regarding what they understand to be acceptable and scriptural.

3. There must be "oneness" before a husband and wife can open up sexually.

Genesis 2:24 (NIV) reads, "For this reason a man will leave his father and mother and be united to his wife, and they will become one flesh." Leaving and cleaving are essential to the survival of a marriage. When I perform marriage ceremonies, often I admonish the bride and groom to say goodbye to family and friends. They must leave family and friends and cleave to one another.

More often than not, newlywed couples bring too many people into their bedroom. They bring role expectations learned from parents. They bring single friends who are not trying to fight the good fight of staying married. They bring former partners and memories of their uninhibited sexual encounters. They bring seared pornographic images that an unassuming spouse could never measure up against. They bring the misinformation or non-information of parental influence into the bedroom. So in order to give the marriage a fair chance they must choose to leave and cleave. Once you enter a marriage covenant, you are married to your spouse only—not your mother, your father, or your former spouse or your former lover. You need to get them all out of your bedroom!

4. God wants married couples to have sex.

"Certainly—but only within a certain context. It's good for a man to have a wife, and for a woman to have a husband. Sexual drives are strong, but marriage is strong enough to contain them and provide for a balanced and fulfilling sexual life in a world of sexual disorder. The marriage bed must be a place of mutuality—the husband seeking to satisfy his wife, the wife seeking to satisfy her husband. Marriage is not a place to 'stand up for your rights.' Marriage is a decision to serve the other, whether in bed or out. Abstaining from sex is permissible for a period of time if you both agree to it, and if it's for the purposes of prayer and fasting—but only for such times. Then come back together again. Satan has an ingenious way of tempting us when we least expect it" (1 Corinthians 7:2-5, MSG).

The only way to "affair proof" your marriage is to make sure your sex life is solid. Make a conscious decision to serve your spouse, both in bed and out. It is wrong to deny your spouse sexually. The only times you should deny one another is for mutual times of prayer, and even then for only a short time so that the devil won't come in and tempt you.

The amazing thing about this Scripture passage is that Satan is at work here—not in sex, but in the absence of it. Satan first tempted Eve when she was separated from her man. Now, a woman and man cannot be joined at the hip always, and God has given women the ability to make sound decisions just as He has given men. Nevertheless, the symbolism is rich. It was while they were separated that the devil had room to come in. The only time a man and a woman ought to be separated from sexual intimacy should be when they are concentrating on spiritual intimacy. When a husband and wife remain together, the devil has no room to come in.

In their book, *Couples Who Pray,* Squire Rushnell and Louse Duart discover something amazing about prayer and sex. There are distinct differences when comparing couples who pray together sometimes versus those who pray together often:

- 67 percent versus 82 percent—an elevation of 15 percent—report they are satisfied with their sex life "a very great deal" or "a great deal."

- 52 percent versus 72 percent—20 percent more—say both the quantity and quality of their lovemaking is "very good."

- 69 percent versus 78 percent—apply the term "ecstasy" to their lovemaking.

- 42 percent versus 63 percent—say, "My spouse is romantic."

- 48 percent versus 65 percent—contend, "My spouse is a skillful lover."

- 49 percent versus 68 percent—"feel spiritual joy after lovemaking."

Clearly, this research shows there is great benefit to couples praying together. Greeley's analysis of the Gallup study concluded: "Prayer...is a much more powerful predictor of marital satisfaction than frequency of sexual intercourse—though the combination of sex and prayer correlates with very, very high levels of marital fulfillment."

5. Don't call anything nasty that God has made clean.

Peter learned this lesson: "About noon the following day as they were on their journey and approaching the city, Peter went up on the roof to pray. He became hungry and wanted something to eat, and while the meal was being prepared, he fell into a trance. He saw heaven opened and something like a large sheet being let down to earth by its four corners. It contained all kinds of four-footed animals, as well as reptiles of the earth and birds of the air. Then a voice told him, 'Get up, Peter. Kill and eat.' 'Surely not, Lord!' Peter replied. 'I have never eaten anything impure or unclean.' The voice spoke to him a second time, 'Do not call anything impure that God has made clean'" (Acts 10:9-15, NIV).

Because of tradition, partly based on a distorted understanding of Puritan values, many Christians feel that it is "nasty" to discuss sex. Further, there are certain acts that many Christians often debate as "nasty." Practices such as oral sex, anal sex, masturbation, and using sex toys are denigrated, all because someone deemed them as unclean. However, there is no explicit condemnation of these activities in the bedroom of married couples. The man and the woman must agree upon what is acceptable, but to call certain acts unclean when God has sanctified the bedroom of married couples is not acceptable. Couples miss out on a great deal of pleasure "between the sheets" because they have a misconception that certain sexual practices are unclean because it originates from a "Gentile" menu.

Christian couples should strive to broaden their menu options after they have spent considerable time talking and praying about what is acceptable in their bedroom. Explicit activities like homosexuality, incest, and adultery (swinging) are expressly prohibited in the Bible—but others, like oral sex and anal sex, are not mentioned and must be negotiated among spouses.

[handwritten margin notes: "Mark 10:8" and "It should bring pleasure + not pain to either." and "to both gives"]

6. God wants spouses to admire each other's body.

The Man:

"You're so beautiful, my darling, so beautiful, and your
    dove eyes are veiled
By your hair as it flows and shimmers,
like a flock of goats in the distance
streaming down a hillside in the sunshine.
Your smile is generous and full—
expressive and strong and clean.
Your lips are jewel red,
your mouth elegant and inviting,
your veiled cheeks soft and radiant.
The smooth, lithe lines of your neck
command notice—all heads turn in awe and admiration!
Your breasts are like fawns,
twins of a gazelle, grazing among the first spring flowers.
The sweet, fragrant curves of your body,
the soft, spiced contours of your flesh
Invite me, and I come. I stay
until dawn breathes its light and night slips away.
You're beautiful from head to toe, my dear love,
beautiful beyond compare, absolutely flawless"

Song of Solomon 4 (MSG).

Who said couples have to make love with the lights off? God gave us beautiful bodies to adore, yet many people feel the naked human body is something to be ashamed of. The problem is that many people have a poor self-image when it comes to their physical appearance. It is difficult to be naked and unashamed when you believe your naked body is unattractive or a source of shame.

7. Each spouse's body belongs to the other.

The husband should not deprive his wife of sexual intimacy, which is her right as a married woman, nor should the wife deprive her husband.

The wife gives authority over her body to her husband, and the husband also gives authority over his body to his wife (see 1 Corinthians 7:34).

When you are married, your body is no longer your possession. You must be in constant communication with your spouse as to when you want sexual access to each other. This sexual connection is also spiritual. Something spiritual takes place when a man enters a woman—they become one. That is why Paul said (in 1 Corinthians 6:15-17, NIV): "Do you not know that your bodies are members of Christ himself? Shall I then take the members of Christ and unite them with a prostitute? Never! Do you not know that he who unites himself with a prostitute is one with her in body? For it is said, 'The two will become one flesh.' But he who unites himself with the Lord is one with him in spirit."

Because sex is a spiritual connection as well as a physical union, it especially must be guarded. Only those who have been sanctified, or "set apart" should be allowed to enter into God's sanctuary. Remember that in 1 Corinthians 6:19 (NIV), the apostle Paul cautioned, "Do you not know that your body is a temple of the Holy Spirit?" Your body is a temple and your spouse is the priest who has been ordained to enter into the sanctuary. When anyone other than a priest tried to enter the holy of holies that person was killed. When you allow someone other than your priest (spouse) to enter in, you bring death to your marriage. Too many Christian marriages are on life support, at the brink of death, because either spouse has allowed a third party to enter the sanctuary.

"The priests are to keep my requirements so that they do not become guilty and die for treating them with contempt. I am the LORD, who makes them holy" (Leviticus 22:9, NIV). Just as the Lord expected His priests to keep His commandments with all diligence, you should strive with equal fervor to protect the sanctity of your marriage bed.

Sexual Immorality Explained

What is sexual immorality? One commentator defines it as *koitē*, which literally means "a bed," and has within its meaning the desire for the forbidden bed. This was the typical heathen sin. The word brings to mind the man who places no value on fidelity and who takes his pleasure when and where he will. This commentator understands a sexually immoral person as someone who has no discretion when it comes to being pleased sexually. He or she is not faithful to the marriage covenant. The sexually immoral person is preoccupied by the "forbidden bed," that which is not sanctioned by God, and yields him- or herself to any and all desires.

Strong's Exhaustive Concordance translates the Greek word immorality as "adultery, fornication, homosexuality, lesbianism, intercourse with animals, etc.; sexual intercourse with close relatives; (see Leviticus 18) sexual intercourse with a divorced man or woman; or the worship of idols (see Mark 10:11; 12:2).

Spouses who have been raised in a conservative upbringing might struggle with what they believe is "immoral." Sexual immorality is clearly spelled out in Strong's interpretation of the original biblical languages as "any kind of sexual activity with anyone other than your spouse." Even when the marriage bed is undefiled there are guidelines that Christians must abide by as it relates to sexually moral behavior and sexually immoral behavior in order to maintain harmony in the marital bed. Some types of sexual activity may be acceptable to some couples while others might consider them sexually immoral:

Oral Sex—One of the most romantic books of the Bible, Song of Songs, mentions oral sex: "Like an apple tree among the trees of the forest is my lover among the young men. I delight to sit in his shade, and his fruit is sweet to my taste" (Song 2:3, NIV). One day, I asked my wife if women in the church thought that oral sex was immoral. She said that some probably do. I asked, "Why?" She explained that it is because oral sex has been associated with what whores or prostitutes do for their clients, something no "decent" woman would do. It is what rappers tell "female dogs" to do in their misogynistic lyrics. When these negative images are brought into the bedroom, the woman makes the association that she is being asked to degrade her "virtuous" identity for that of an average "street" woman.

The truth of the matter is that oral sex is mentioned in Scripture as part of the menu of a healthy sexual appetite. The late comedian Bernie Mac, in his infamous Kings of Comedy performance, made fun of his wife Rhonda when he said, "When you get married, oral sex stops. Your wife pretends like she doesn't know what she's doing so that you will tell her to stop. I don't tell her to stop, I tell her to keep going. 'You need the practice!'"

Women and men both need the practice because for the longest both have associated something "nasty" with touching their lips to the genitalia of their spouses. With proper hygiene, oral sex can be one of the more pleasurable experiences of committed, disease-free, married couples; but they must make the mental paradigm shift regarding oral sex from nasty to delectable fruit.

Anal Sex—Many conservative Christians like to use the destruction of Sodom and Gomorrah (see Genesis 18–19) as a proof text to condemn anal sex. The men's desire to rape Lot's guests was what enraged God, not anal sex between a husband and a wife. Although the anus is very sensitive, and sexually arousing for some, anal/rectal tissue is delicate and is not designed to expand in the same way as vaginal tissue.

As with oral sex, couples need to determine what is acceptable behavior for them. Should both spouses agree, care needs to be taken during anal play and lots of lubrication is essential.

Lingerie/costumes—Marriage is forever; therefore, variety is needed to spice up what can become routine. As a pastor, I have suits in all of the basic colors. One of the ways I make my suits look new or different is because I have a variety of neckties. Some people think I have on a new suit when all I have done is changed the accessories to something I wear all the time.

You can add spice to your marriage by accessorizing the body your spouse sees all the time. Lingerie, or even costumes, takes the sexual experience out of the routine and expected and creates anticipation that enhances sexual experiences beyond the usual and perfunctory.

Some acts are not a matter of choice between a husband and wife; they are expressly prohibited in the Word of God.

Pornography (lust for others, mental adultery)—"Pornography, the tired utterance of harlots, is like the refrigerator of blues song: it can't keep anything. So it spoils by leaving nothing for imagination to imagine. Privacy is negated as pornography invites the world to stare into the bedrooms of our soul."

Jesus teaches in Luke 11:33-35 (NIV): "No one lights a lamp and puts it in a place where it will be hidden, or under a bowl. Instead he puts it on its stand, so that those who come in may see the light. Your eye is the lamp of your body. When your eyes are good, your whole body also is full of light. But when they are bad, your body also is full of darkness. See to it, then, that the light within you is not darkness."

Men, being visual creatures, are especially susceptible to the addictive grip of pornography. The more a man feeds his flesh with these captivating visual images the more he slides into addiction and away from sexual purity. According to Stephen Arterburn, in his book, *Every Man's Battle*, sexual purity is when a man is sexually gratified with his wives only. He also says that men receive a chemical high from sexually charged images. At the sight of these images, a hormone called epinephrine is secreted into his bloodstream, which locks into his memory whenever stimulus is present at the time of the emotional excitement.

Adultery—Matthew 5:27-28 (NIV): "You have heard that it was said, 'Do not commit adultery.' But I tell you that anyone who looks at a woman lustfully has already committed adultery with her in his heart." Jesus admonishes His hearers because He knew there are many ways adultery or adulterous thoughts can damage a marriage. In addition to the garden-variety infidelity, a lot has been discussed lately about online affairs. This epidemic has compromised countless marriages and caused a number of divorces.

Although there is no physical intimacy, an online affair involves the same kinds of emotions as physical affairs do—deception, secrecy, fantasy, and the sense of forbidden excitement, along with rationalization for what you do and denial of the effects. An online affair is potentially as devastating as a physical affair. *Ladies & their emotional affairs*

Sometimes spouses get caught up in emotional affairs, perhaps with a co-worker or even a church member. While there is no exchange of physical intimacies, both parties involved begin to develop feelings and engage in the same types of deception as an actual physical infidelity.

Then there is the traditional affair—the "clean-up woman" or the "Jody" who is always on standby, waiting for the inevitable crack in a troubled marriage. Carl was in active search of a mistress, and he often lured them with talk of the trappings of his success, telling women about his large home and his good job. Although he had no intention of leaving his wife (probably for financial reasons), he was looking for intimacy with a third party. His usual response was, "Sometimes you just need somebody." He found a way to justify his infidelity. He and his wife were staying together so they wouldn't have to divide the assets of a twenty-year marriage.

Swinging (adultery)—Leviticus 20:10 (NIV) reads, "'If a man commits adultery with another man's wife—with the wife of his neighbor—both the adulterer and the adulteress must be put to death."

While swinging is absent of the lies and deception that accompany tradition and online affairs, introducing a third party into a marriage can still open the door to all kinds of emotional land mines. One movie comes to mind, Indecent Proposal, in which a rich man offers a man one million dollars to sleep with his wife. The man and his wife accepted the proposal but the incident was far from over after the sexual encounter. The man and his wife were torn emotionally when he asked her, "Was he better than me?" She screamed, "Yes! Is that what you want to hear?" A great deal came with that million dollars—much pain, the threat of divorce, and years of rebuilding. Many couples don't have Hollywood endings to a marriage that has been torn by infidelity; all they have is the pain, mistrust, anger, and suffering.

Menage-a-trois (*threesomes—swapping, adultery, homosexuality, orgies*)—Leviticus 18:22 (NIV): "Do not lie with a man as one lies with a woman; that is detestable." When couples feel the need to add spice by adding people to their bedroom, they multiply the consequences of defiling their marriage bed. As believers, we cannot bring worldly practices into our bedroom. Many of the so-called "sex improvement" or "self-help" books explore all kinds of fantasies and sex play that are not in keeping with what God says about sexually acceptable behaviors.

Orgies are not part of God's plan for the marriage bed. Romans 13:13 (NIV) reads: "Let us behave decently, as in the daytime, not in orgies and drunkenness, not in sexual immorality and debauchery, not in dissension and jealousy." When you give in to sexual behavior that is in clear violation of God's Word, it can lead you to the point where you don't care that you are hurting God and hurting yourself. You become numb to your behavior, or what the Bible calls "reprobate." Plus, your plan can backfire on you. There have been many instances where a man wanted to watch his wife have sex with another woman, only to have his wife fall in love with the other woman and leave him. She exchanges her natural desire for her husband for an unnatural desire for another woman.

Paul cautioned in Romans 1:26-27 (NIV): "Because of this, God gave them over to shameful lusts. Even their women exchanged natural relations for unnatural ones. In the same way the men also abandoned natural relations with women and were inflamed with lust for one another. Men committed indecent acts with other men, and received in themselves the due penalty for their perversion."

In the movie *The Sex Monster* (1999), Mariel Hemingway plays a wife whose husband goads her into a threesome with another woman. Soon, the man finds himself left out of the sex play that the two women begin to indulge in regularly. She soon moves from the first lover to a series of female encounters. The film's tagline is "the ultimate male fantasy gets a reality check." While billed as a comedy, the husband was hardly laughing by the time it was over.

Similarly, there has been much talk about men on the "down low" openly engaged in a heterosexual relationship while privately participating in homosexual encounters. Living a double life places a strain on the marriage, in addition to the hurt, lies, and deceptions necessary to live such a lifestyle. Couples cannot live naked and unashamed if either spouse is engaged in deceptive behaviors.

There are many gray areas for some Christian couples—like romance novels, masturbation, and sex toys—that cloud their judgment and muddy the waters of sexual intimacy. These are matters for the couples to address among themselves. Keep in mind, however, how the apostle Paul talked to the Corinthian church about food sacrificed to idols: "But food does not bring us near to God; we are no worse if we do not eat, and no better if we do. Be careful, however, that the exercise of your freedom does not become a stumbling block to the weak" (1 Corinthians 8:8-9, NIV).

Now if the word food were substituted for "vibrator," for example, the same argument could be used. We could say, "Porn stars use vibrators for entertainment and their lifestyle is contrary to the Word of God, but as a married Christian I also know that a vibrator can give my wife extra stimulation to bring her to orgasm. Am I to abandon something useful in my marriage bed because an unbeliever uses a similar device?"

Paul's argument is that if you know God does not explicitly condemn participating in an activity, then you should use your good conscience and be free to incorporate that in your diet. But if you are participating in something that may offend someone weaker in the faith, then you should not flaunt your freedom for fear of causing others to stumble in their weaker faith. So if going to an adult bookstore to buy "adult toys" will offend some of your Christian brothers and sisters or confuse non-believers, then perhaps you should order online.

Ultimately, the decision of what you bring into your bedroom is a matter of prayer, communication, the reading of God's Word, and common sense. What one couple considers moral and immoral can become subjective because what that couple agrees to will differ from another Christian couple's agreement. To be objective, open, and honest, both spouses must carefully search the Scriptures and their hearts to see what agrees with their spirits and their sexual appetite.

Talk about sex with your children in the context of God. It's done in the sight of God.

And no creature is hidden
from his sight, but all are naked
and exposed to the eyes of
him to whom we must give account.
Hebrews 4:13 (ESV)

CHAPTER TWO
Invite God into Your Bedroom

*H*usband and wife duo Kenny Latimore and Chante Moore released a CD entitled *Uncovered*. When they were interviewed about the project on the Word Channel, Latimore said they wanted to do a CD with two discs. The first disc would contain romantic love songs and the second would contain love songs to Jesus, or what we call in the church "praise songs." He commented, "It's time for us to talk about the whole person as it relates to love in a Christian marriage and who we are in Christ."

This is an interesting concept for these two former R&B Christian singers. The veil between the secular and the sacred has always been thin in the African-American church. Our theology of the sacred and the secular can be traced back to the life-altering sacrifice of Jesus when He died for our sins on the cross. The Bible records in Matthew 27:51 (NIV), "At that moment the curtain of the temple was torn in two from top to bottom. The earth shook and the rocks split." The curtain separated the Holy of Holies from the common people. His death allowed us direct access to the Holy. No more separation. We were covered, but uncovered.

African spirituality does not separate God into compartments. When I traveled to Ghana, West Africa, I noticed that there were stores with names like Thank You, Jesus Grocery or Glory Garage. The people sang praise songs while they worked; their spirituality permeates their everyday lives. This African tradition has been with us through the evolution of black music, with the likes of Sam Cooke and Aretha Franklin (who grew up in church), and the same passion they have singing for God was felt when they sang their love songs.

This blended approach by Kenny and Chante' is a breath of fresh air because Christians have struggled with bringing the two worlds of God's agape love into their bedroom, where there is Eros. In his book *The Four Loves*, C. S. Lewis talks about Eros. He differentiates between the animalistic passion of Eros and the more spiritually wholesome aspect of Eros. He says that the animalistic passion of Eros, known as Venus, is more concerned with the act of sex, whereas the true Eros is concerned with the beloved. However, Lewis concedes that Eros is needed for a successful Christian marriage.

Dr. Reginald Martin, in *Dark Eros*, discusses the holistic value of Eros as it relates to African sexuality. He believes that when Eros is experienced and people come in touch with their erotic self they move toward authenticity. However, he warns that Eros is not an end in itself. When the erotic nature comes to the heart of Eros, all is known. Eros is of God, but not God. Eros is a blessing.[1]

The older, moral theologians seem to have thought that the danger we chiefly had to guard against in marriage was a soul-destroying surrender to the senses. The couples, whose marriages would certainly be endangered, and possibly ruined, are those who have idolized Eros. They thought they had the power and truthfulness of a god. They expected that mere feeling would do all that was necessary for them to build a lasting and permanent union. When this expectation is disappointed, they throw the blame on Eros, or more usually, on their partners. In reality, however, Eros, having made his gigantic promise and shown you in glimpses what its performance would be like, has "done his stuff." He, like a godparent, makes the vows; it is we who must keep them.

It is we who must labor to bring our daily life into even closer accord with what the glimpses of Eros have revealed. We must do the work of Eros when Eros is not present. And all good Christian lovers know that this program, modest as it sounds, will not be carried out except by humility, charity, and divine grace; that it is, indeed, the whole Christian life seen from one particular angle.

Best-selling author and psychologist M. Scott Peck observed that "falling in love" is God's way of "tricking" human beings into marriage—thus ensuring procreation and stability within our society. He noted that if people entered into marriage absent of feeling love and Eros, most would never walk down the aisle because the reality of what marriage really entails would be too great.

It is shared in Hebrews 4:13 how all creation is uncovered/naked before God. Whether we can admit it or not, we are already naked before God. Everything is uncovered before Him. Human nakedness was designed to be a blessing and not a curse. When we are in right relationship with God, we are uncovered and unashamed. The goal of every married couple is to get back to being uncovered. Their aim is to get back to a holistic, erotic love that involves the erotic and agape love of God.

Being a Christian who is married means more than being a one-dimensional praiser. In fact, the more passionate one is about praising God, the more praise should show up in one's bedroom toward his or her spouse. David was a praiser. He praised God so much that he danced right out of his clothes. His wife Michal became indignant because she thought he was showing out in front of the young women. David had to remind his wife that he was not showing out for the women but was, rather, expressing his appreciation to God.

It is easy for the line to be blurred when it comes to spirituality versus sensuality. A healthy relationship has a good blend of both. Often the distinction is forced by observers who are not in right relationship with

God and are uncomfortable with their own nakedness. Michal, David's estranged wife, was bitter because David had forced himself back into her life after years of separation. When there is emotional separation between a man and a woman it is hard for them to connect and appreciate being uncovered.

The Bible states that Michal was barren the rest of her days. There are a lot of marriages that are barren because the man and woman fail to connect emotionally or one spouse cannot appreciate the passionate fervor of the other. He or she is offended by the other's "uncoveredness." Patti Labelle sang in "If You Don't Know Me by Now":

"Does my sexiness offend you,
the way my clothes fall off me?
Honey, if that's it you ain't worth me no how."

Toward a Healthy Blend

Married couples ought to be able to explore their nakedness with one another without shame. In the past, sex has been limited to procreation with recreation being permissible within that context. Sex has a greater purpose than procreation. Sexual intimacy is a way for couples to connect spiritually and emotionally. Sex is a way to bring both worlds, the secular and the sacred, together.

Bishop T. D. Jakes has made a wonderful attempt at blending the two in his production of a Christian CD, *Sacred Love Songs*. I have to admit that when I first heard of the concept, I had some cognitive dissonance because I was stuck in the old mindset of the two being separated. This separateness causes conflict in our psyche because we have not reconciled our two selves.

Dr. James Hollis addresses this tension in his book, *Why Good People Do Bad Things*. He writes, "Wholeness can never be approached without the embrace of the opposites. Indeed, the wholeness embodied in "the self" is made manifest in the opposites and in the conflict between them…Hence, the way to the self begins with conflict."

One couple in particular in our marriage workshop had an issue with the sacredness of sex. One husband said, "Pastor, when my wife and I make love, she likes to say, 'Oh hell.'" I responded, "Hell is in the Bible." He said, "That doesn't bother me as much as when she says, 'Oh God!'" The crowd erupted with laughter.

I told the brother that his wife calling on God was an act of worship. She was thankful for the sacred union between a husband and a wife. The conflict came from them making love and his wife calling on God. When you are married, sex is a sacred moment and there should be no psychological conflict while listening to sacred love songs or calling on the name of the Lord. Having sex with your spouse ought to be a time of thanksgiving for being able to enter that sacred place.

Sex between a husband and wife is a sacred act. In the Old Testament, whenever the high priest sacrificed an offering to God, he had to go behind a curtain to enter the Holy of Holies. There he would make a blood sacrifice for the propitiation (atonement) of the sins of the people. When a man and woman consummate their marriage, there is such rich symbolism in the way that a man enters the woman, just as the high priest enters the Holy of Holies. The Jewish people would lay a cloth beneath a newly married couple so they would have proof of the woman's virginity. In this way, the man would have proof that no other man had entered that sacred place.

Outlined in the book of Deuteronomy (22:13-18, NIV) is a procedure for establishing proof of the woman's virginity: "If a man takes a wife and, after lying with her, dislikes her and slanders her and gives her a bad name, saying, 'I married this woman, but when I approached her, I did not find proof of her virginity,' then the girl's father and mother shall bring proof that she was a virgin to the town elders at the gate. The girl's father will say to the elders, 'I gave my daughter in marriage to this man, but he dislikes her. Now he has slandered her and said, '"I did not find your daughter to be a virgin." But here is the proof of my daughter's virginity.' Then her parents shall display the cloth before the elders of the town, and the elders shall take the man and punish him."

The parents' proof was the blood of the broken hymen. When the husband had sex with his wife for the first time, if she was a virgin the hymen would break, causing blood to flow. He was the first to enter in.

Sex is a spiritual act that should be entered into reverently. When you have sex with someone who has been "ordained" or selected by God to enter in, it is a wonderful, sacred moment.

Perversion of the marriage bed has caused many people to have the wrong view of being uncovered. There is a time to be covered and a time to be uncovered. Our society doesn't have a problem with people walking around uncovered. We are by no means a modest society by far. In the eastern tradition, particularly with Muslim women, the females are covered from head to toe because they believe that only their husbands should have the privilege of seeing their skin.

In 1 Corinthians 11:5-6 (NIV), Paul spoke about women having their heads covered in worship. "And every woman who prays or prophesies with her head uncovered dishonors her head—it is just as though her head were shaved. If a woman does not cover her head, she should have her hair cut off; and if it is a disgrace for a woman to have her hair cut or shaved off, she should cover her head."

Paul was addressing a cultural understanding of what was acceptable in Corinth. The issue was not whether a woman should have her head covered in church but, rather, that she be subordinated to her husband. During those times, a woman's hair was her glory that only her husband should see. For a woman in Corinth to have her head uncovered was equivalent to her saying, "My husband is not the head of our house, I am." This issue was about the man covering the woman, not what the woman used to cover her head.

As extreme as this example seems, there is some truth behind the concept of not being uncovered in front of the wrong people. We have taken our freedom as Protestants and Americans to another level. People leave nothing to the imagination when they publicly expose themselves by wearing mini-skirts, g-string bikinis, and see-through blouses.

There is a time to be covered and a time to be uncovered. When I speak of being uncovered or naked it is intended for your spouse only in a sacred place. The perversion comes when people who are not supposed to uncover your nakedness—close relatives and people other than your spouse—get to see something that only your spouse is supposed to see. There are appropriate places for husbands and wives to be uncovered and there are inappropriate places. Spouses must choose wisely where, when, and to whom they allow themselves to be uncovered.

Take Noah for example: "Noah, a man of the soil, proceeded to plant a vineyard. When he drank some of its wine, he became drunk and lay uncovered inside his tent. Ham, the father of Canaan, saw his father's nakedness and told his two brothers outside. But Shem and Japheth took a garment and laid it across their shoulders; then they walked in backward and covered their father's nakedness. Their faces were turned the other way so that they would not see their father's nakedness" (Genesis 9:20-23, NIV).

Leviticus 18 is very clear about whose nakedness we should not uncover. There are some people we have no business seeing uncovered. Ham's mistake was not accidentally seeing his father naked; rather, his sin was exposing his father's nakedness by telling his brothers. The brothers respectfully walked in backwards and covered their father. Ham didn't cover his father. Sometimes people leave their loved ones uncovered.

Indeed, Noah was drunk. Sometimes people can allow the wrong ones to see them exposed because of their own intoxication. When a person is sober and alert, he or she will not be uncovered by the wrong people. "Covering" is an intimate responsibility not to be taken lightly. Ham should have covered Noah; instead, he made a joke about his father's nakedness.

A married person should protect his or her spouse's vulnerability. When spouses can be naked and unashamed with each other, each has the security of knowing the other spouse is watching his or her back. When one spouse commits adultery, that spouse is exposing his or her nakedness, and the other spouse's nakedness as well. When one spouse talks to family or friends about what goes on in their bedroom, that spouse has exposed the other spouse's nakedness as well. No one else should have a mental image of what is designed for the spouse's eyes only.

There is something sacred about nakedness. It is not designed to entertain everyone. Ham failed to cover the sacredness of his father's nakedness. Every couple should be careful not to expose what goes on in their bedroom.

A man can go to work and confide in the wrong person about what's going on in his bedroom. He may encounter the proverbial adulteress at work who is just waiting to hear his latest story about how his wife is just not "feeling" him at home. If the temptress has set her sights on him, she can flip the situation and start telling him what she would do if she were his woman. He may not be able to resist the temptation. That's why the nature of a couple's sex life should be kept sacred and confidential.

A similar marital disaster can happen if a woman who is very satisfied at home starts telling her girlfriends about how her man is "handling his business" at home. Each time the girlfriends see him they become friendlier and friendlier to her husband. One of the so-called friends may even show up at the house while the wife is not home, hoping the husband can give her the same treatment. The nature of a couple's sex life—whether good or bad—should not be shared outside their bedroom.

This same argument about letting outsiders into the bedroom holds true for pornography also. A couple attending our marriage workshop wanted to know whether it is acceptable to use pornography in enhancing their sex life. I told them that the danger of pornography is that it may lead to a desire for other outlets that could take them beyond the boundaries of marital sacredness. The desire for pornography is often progressive and the need for more bizarre visual sensations comes over time. My advice to the couple was that if they wanted to see some naked people, they could make a tape of themselves for themselves. If a couple makes a tape or takes pictures of their own sexual activity, that tape is for their eyes only. It is sacred.

Pulling the Covers Back

Husbands and wives have every right to live their lives uncovered. It is time for married couples to pull back the covers on their full sexuality. Often when young people think about getting married, they think about a restricted institution where sex becomes routine and mechanical. What they do not know is that sex between a Christian husband and wife can be just as romantic and passionate as what some of the R&B singers profess in their music. The difference is that all of that raw passion is channeled into a committed relationship that is sealed by the hand of God. There are erotic desires and passions trapped in many Christian bodies that never get expressed because people are covered up. They have layers of shame that will not allow them to express fully who they are. Many couples are "sexually starved" because they don't know how to reveal who they really are and what they really want.

I recall a particular young couple in our church that was sexually repressed. I'll call them Calvin and Lisa. Calvin had already had an affair in their young marriage. He had come from a holy background and nobody had ever talked to either one of them about sex. They had major inhibitions regarding nudity and what was acceptable, even between a husband and wife.

Lisa also had her share of hang-ups. She wanted to wear some sexy lingerie, but the husband didn't think it was necessary. When they made love she would wear flannel or cotton pajamas or an old T-shirt, and they would leave the lights off. My wife began to coach Lisa on how to make herself more appealing to her husband. She began to wear sexy lingerie to bed and the rest is history. She traded in her jogging pants for some lace panties and now they leave the lights on.

We have not reconciled all of who we are when we have compartmentalized ourselves into sacred and secular. Often men are more given to compartmentalizing parts of their lives, which is why it is often easier for a man to have sex outside the marriage but still claim to love his wife.

We in the church have established our own regulations about what is sexual and what is sacred—women not being able to wear pants to church, no red lipstick, no makeup, no bathing suits, and so forth. Ironically, the greatest degree of sexual promiscuity and out-of-wedlock pregnancy can be found in some of these "holiness" faith traditions. The people within these traditions don't know what to do with all of the passion they have been taught to keep covered up.

It is time for the church to deal with the whole person. Engaged young couples should be taught in pre-marital counseling how to set an atmosphere for a romantic evening. Young women should be taught that men are visual creatures who need variety; therefore, it is okay not to keep Victoria a secret. Young men can be taught how to be romantic and that women only want sex after they feel they have been cared for and listened to.

Young couples planning to marry should be taught about their bodies and how to explore every part of their temples. The church must remove this curtain that separates cute Christian talk about marriage and the erotic volcano waiting to erupt. The marriage bed can handle any kind of passions of these young couples produce once they have been taught how to remove their shame associated with being sexual beings.

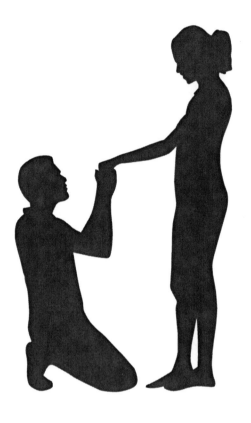

*How the king of Israel has
distinguished himself today,
disrobing in the sight of
the slave girls of his servants
as any vulgar fellow would!"
(2 Samuel 6:20, NIV)*

CHAPTER THREE
Why Did I Get Married?

"When David returned home to bless his household, Michal daughter of Saul came out to meet him and said, 'How the king of Israel has distinguished himself today, disrobing in the sight of the slave girls of his servants as any vulgar fellow would!' David said to Michal, 'It was before the LORD, who chose me rather than your father or anyone from his house when he appointed me ruler over the LORD's people Israel—I will celebrate before the LORD. I will become even more undignified than this, and I will be humiliated in my own eyes. But by these slave girls you spoke of, I will be held in honor.' And Michal daughter of Saul had no children to the day of her death" (2 Samuel 6:20-23, NIV).

It is amazing how people can fall in love with each other and want to spend the rest of their lives together. Then, just a few years later they feel as though they are two strangers living under the same roof. Each of them may ask, "Why did I get married?"

Writer/producer Tyler Perry delivered an instant cinematic hit encompassing that very question. In the movie, he profiles the relationships of four couples that could have been anybody in America. The movie deals with issues that are fairly common to contemporary marriages—

infidelity, self-esteem, respect, deception, lack of communication, inhibitions, and the need for forgiveness. Each couple in the movie had to answer their own question regarding the state of their marriage. The issues they were in conflict about were never really dealt with until all of their secrets were revealed.

Marriage is challenging, even in the best relationships. So, if marriage can be so difficult, why do people get married? Let's examine some reasons.

1. To Be Free from Parents (Genesis 2:23-25)

"And Adam said, This is now bone of my bones, and flesh of my flesh: she shall be called Woman, because she was taken out of Man. Therefore shall a man leave his father and his mother, and shall cleave unto his wife: and they shall be one flesh. And they were both naked, the man and his wife, and were not ashamed" (KJV).

Getting married just to escape from home is not a good reason. Sherry got married for just that reason. She had flunked out of college and wasn't particularly interested in college anyway. She couldn't find a job that would pay her enough money to live on her own. Then she met Barry, who had a good job and was pretty much willing to do whatever she wanted. Even before the wedding, she had misgivings, but her parents had already spent a great deal of money on the fantasy wedding she wanted. So she married him and they bought a house.

After about three years of marriage, she decided to have a baby, thinking that would strengthen her interest in and commitment to the marriage. After the initial excitement of having a baby wore off and the responsibilities wore on, Sherry began having extramarital affairs. She refused to divorce because, just like when she married, she didn't earn enough money to make it on her on, plus she didn't want to give up the house they'd purchased. After twelve years of an unfulfilling marriage, Sherry filed for divorce. When she reflected on the entire marriage, she admitted that her motivation for the marriage was wrong from the beginning and that her decision to stay in it for the wrong reasons had been detrimental to them both.

Before you can become successfully married you need to be successfully single. I remember getting married at a very young age, having never really lived on my own, and the struggles related to making the adjustment. Each young adult should get a full experience of what it feels like to be independent. A person has to know self and love self before he or she can commit to another.

2. Sex Without Guilt (1 Corinthians 7:9)

Getting married just to have sex can be a big disappointment because marriage cannot be built on sex alone. Christians, especially those from conservative religious backgrounds, are especially prone to seeking "legal sex" through marriage. Human beings cannot live on sex alone and a relationship cannot survive on sexual activity, no matter how intense. That is why the dating process should be a time of building a strong foundation of friendship and self-discovery—finding out what a person likes and dislikes in a mate.

Carmen entered a sexual relationship soon after meeting Jason. The sex was intense and their desire for one another was strong. They both began to think they were falling in love and possibly had the makings of a lasting relationship. After a couple of months, however, Carmen began to notice more about Jason's character. After the third month, she began to realize that she and Jason did not share the same values and that she really didn't like him much as a person. She had to admit to herself that her judgment was clouded by great sex and that she compromised herself by sharing what should have been sacred with someone who wasn't worthy.

When sex does not dominate the relationship, a person can focus on major issues of compatibility—issues that make or break a relationship. When two people get married, good sex is a natural result of having established the right foundation, not the other way around.

3. To Ease Loneliness (Ecclesiastes 4:11)

"Also, if two lie down together, they will keep warm. But how can one keep warm alone?" (NIV).

Jill Scott has a song on her latest CD, *The Real Thing: Words and Sounds, Volume 3*, entitled "I'm Lonely Whenever You Are Around." She is singing about a husband who is treating her coldly by being emotionally distant and keeping her at arms length. When people get married, they should go into marriage realizing that there will be times in the marriage when they feel disconnected. This phenomenon will be discussed more in the chapter on tension between Adam and Eve.

Each spouse must learn the art of being content with self because even in the best marriages each must appreciate himself or herself alone so that when they come together it is even sweeter.

4. To Be Happy (Ecclesiastes 9:9)

"Enjoy life with your wife, whom you love, all the days of this meaningless life that God has given you under the sun—all your meaningless days. For this is your lot in life and in your toilsome labor under the sun" (NIV).

This is a dangerous move—marrying in an attempt to make yourself happy. I've listened to so many young married people talk about wanting to get a divorce because they are not happy. Marriage is not a continuous journey of ecstasy, fulfillment, and joy. Happiness is based on conditions; it is based on external circumstances. And when conditions change, so does the feeling of happiness that was sought through the marriage.

Webster's Dictionary defines "happy" in the following ways:

1. Characterized by good luck; fortunate.
2. Enjoying, showing, or marked by pleasure, satisfaction, or joy.
3. Being especially well-adapted; felicitous: a happy turn of phrase.
4. Cheerful; willing: happy to help.

All of these definitions are conditional and dependent on external circumstances. Christians don't believe in living a pleasure-centered life. We live for something far greater in meaning and purpose.

A pleasure-centered approach to marriage naturally leads to a desire to exit the marriage when spouses feel they are not receiving the bliss expected out of the relationship. When pleasure is the primary focus in marriage, it is easy to abandon the commitment in search of someone who can spontaneously make the person happy. The hard part is staying in a lackluster marriage and searching for ways to make each other happier.

Raymond wasn't satisfied with his wife. The thrill was long-gone. They seemed to have separate interests and hobbies. They rarely went anywhere together and sex was a non-issue. All they had in common were their kids and their bills. He thought often about divorce, but the prospect of unraveling seventeen years of marriage seemed overwhelming. He sort of felt like that phrase from the seventies song by Gladys Knight and the Pips epitomized his life: "Neither one of us wants to be the first to say goodbye."

Raymond was very unfulfilled sexually and was beginning to feel very unnecessary at home. He was starting to think about Robin, a cute, sexy woman he saw frequently at the gym. Every time he saw her she was happy and greeted him with a smile. They often had long talks in the parking lot. They talked about exciting stuff, not kids and bills and problems. More and more, he fantasized about how being with Robin would make him happy. He started wondering if he should invite her for a bite to eat after a workout some evening.

Like so many spouses, Raymond had begun to expend energy on how to pursue another woman rather than focusing on improving the quality of his marriage.

5. To Be an Adult

According to the Boston Herald, research indicates that people who live together prior to getting married are more likely to have marriages that end in divorce. It is interesting that people who live together prior to getting married often use the defense that they are "grown." In actuality, they are "playing house," because they can leave any time things don't go the way they want. "Shacking up" isn't just a moral offense against the institution of marriage; statistically it doesn't work.

Grandmama said it best: "Why buy the cow when you can get the milk for free?" That's the reason why a man may live with a woman for years and be unwilling to marry her, giving her excuses like "marriage is just a piece of paper" or "I treat you just like my wife already." Yet, after living with that woman for years, that same man will meet another woman and marry her almost instantly.

6. Pregnancy

This is less true in these post-modern times. There used to be a code of ethics that said if a man got a girl pregnant he should do the right thing and marry her. Part of CNN's documentary "Black in America" included a black woman who started a campaign called, "Marry Your Baby Daddy." MaryAnn Reid started this campaign to strengthen two-parent homes and promote marriage and family values. It is an invitation to couples that already live together and have children to legalize their arrangement in the name of love and their community. Many of the couples that married had been together for years, but for a variety of reasons, they had never legalized their relationship.

The likelihood that a woman will eventually marry is significantly lower for those who first had a child out of wedlock. By age thirty-five, only 70 percent of all unwed mothers are married, in contrast to 88 percent of women who have not had a child out of wedlock, according to Lawrence L. Wu and Barbara Wolfe, authors of Finding a Mate? The Marital and Cohabitation Histories of Unwed Mothers.

7. Love (1 Samuel 18:20)

"Now Saul's daughter Michal was in love with David, and when they told Saul about it, he was please" (NIV).

Love is the best reason to get married, but like the sister in the Song of Songs passage, love should not be awakened before it is time. Couples must make sure that their love has matured from Eros (lust) into Agape before saying "I do."

It takes more than love to make a marriage work. Many, many couples who have been in love have divorced—still loving each other.

8. Money (Judges 16:5)

"The rulers of the Philistines went to her and said, 'See if you can lure him into showing you the secret of his great strength and how we can overpower him so we may tie him up and subdue him. Each one of us will give you eleven hundred shekels of silver'" (NIV).

Delilah only wanted Samson for the money she could get, not for his strength or his love for her. Many people only marry for financial security. This holds true for both men and women. Both men and women should be very discerning when choosing a spouse to be sure that the person wants the person and not just his or her resources. As trivial as it seems, some men have married their wives because she owned her own home. Some women have married men because of the man's steady paycheck or high-profile position.

When we fall in love with people who just want us for our money we find ourselves in a bind that could lead to death. Just ask Samson. Conversely, it has wisely been said, "When you marry for money, you earn every penny." Many men and women have sought a wealthy spouse, only to find out that being married to a wealthy mate was not as easy and breezy as they thought.

9. A Lifetime Companion (Genesis 2:18)

"The LORD God said, 'It is not good for the man to be alone. I will make a helper suitable for him'" (NIV).

Human beings are made for companionship. That's why a man or woman would be wise to know that the person he or she desires to marry is the person that God has chosen. The reality, though, is that one person can be compatible with any ten persons in the world. The choice of who to marry should be based on compatibility. Once that choice is made, however, a person must realize that he or she is making a sacrifice to be with that one person for life, even though he or she may cross the path of nine other persons who had the potential to be a "soul mate." The truth is that every person probably is compatible with some other person, or persons. But when God leads two people to each other to marry, each must exercise the discipline of finding all they need in each other.

10. Willingness to Fulfill One Another's Needs and Desires (2 Samuel 6:16)

"And when she (Michal) saw King David leaping and dancing before the LORD, she despised him in her heart" (NIV).

David and Michal loved each other sincerely before the time of this Bible passage. The problem is that they were separated by persecution from Michal's father, Saul. David fled for his life and Saul married his daughter to another man. When David returned and tried to pick up where they left off, things were no longer the same.

There are many couples like David and Michal who really loved each other when they first met but something came between them and caused a separation. Now the separation can occur even though they still live in the same house. Life can separate them. Busy schedules can separate them. Stress can separate them. Goals can separate them. Two people who used to eat each other up now can't even eat together.

In Perry's movie *Why Did I Get Married?*, no one seems to be getting any real love from their spouses. Yes, some are having sex but none of them are making love. Look at their issues as outlined below and see if you are allowing any of these issues to separate you and your spouse.

1. Best-selling author and pop psychologist Patricia (portrayed by Janet Jackson) is doing well on the book circuit, but her marriage to architect Gavin (Malik Yoba) is strained because of the recent death of

their young son in an automobile accident. The death of a child is a traumatic event, and statistically, couples who experience the death of a child are more likely than not to divorce. There can be some traumatic events in our lives where the scars haven't healed. In the case of Patricia and Gavin, they have unresolved grief and blame for the death of their child. Is there anything traumatic that has happened in your marriage that you haven't dealt with? Are you blaming your spouse for something or harboring guilt for something in the past?

2. The second couple is workaholic lawyer Dianne (Sharon Leal) and her neglected and resentful physician husband Terry (Tyler Perry). She avoids intimacy by throwing herself into her work. She's a successful, career-minded spouse who doesn't have time for her man. Fortunately, Terry's a faithful husband. Even though he has a demanding career, he's willing to make time for his marriage. But Dianne does get a wake-up call when she thinks she's about to lose her husband and that someone else wants him. Often it is the husband who neglects the relationship because of work. But in contemporary society, women are just as likely to have a high-powered, demanding position that blinds them to the needs of spouse and family.

3. Then there is the hard-drinking, combative Angela (Tasha Smith) and her loving but cowed and unfaithful husband Marcus (Michael Jai White). Their combined excesses of alcoholism and infidelity were a volatile mix that frequently exploded. She had to commit to avoiding alcohol and he had to "man up" in order for their relationship to survive. Marcus's manhood was constantly challenged by Angela's berating him, reminding him that she was the breadwinner and that he could do little without her. His response was to regain his sense of manhood through infidelity. There are many men trying to prove their manhood by sleeping with a variety of women. Meanwhile, there are many women who are emasculating their husbands with their in-your-face attitudes.

4. Now examine the sweet but overweight and clueless Sheila (Jill Scott) and her verbally abusive husband Mike (Richard T. Jones). Mike was verbally abusive to Sheila and was unfaithful and disrespectful in the worst kinds of ways. Sheila's coping mechanism was to absorb herself in religion. She failed to demand the respect she rightfully

deserved as a wife, no matter what her size. Too many spouses allow themselves to be mistreated and don't command the respect that is rightfully theirs because of low self-esteem. They believe that because of their imperfections or shortcomings, they have no right to demand more in the relationship.

At any given point in their relationship, all married people have struggled with one or more of these issues that cause them to pause—in the midst of neglect, abuse, and infidelity—and ask, "Why did I get married?" Could it be that Patricia and Gavin married for the right reasons? They had expectations that they both had similar goals in life. Everything was going well until their son died in a car accident and Patricia began to bury herself in her work to forget about the guilt she feels over the accident. She blocks intimacy with her husband so they won't have to talk about it. Meanwhile, Gavin loves her, but secretly blames her for not putting on the seat belt.

When we walk around holding in bitterness and resentment, it can cause a chasm that slowly turns a relationship cold. A marriage can survive a traumatic event, but only when the spouses are willing to address it. There is an African proverb that goes, "You cannot heal that which you conceal."

Another danger in relationships is when one spouse is so consumed with career that family comes second. For whatever reason, the spouse's career is primary and the family, particularly the other spouse, gets the leftovers.

What was interesting in this movie is that the roles were reversed. Often it is the man who loses himself in his career and his wife is left clutching the pillow at night. At first I thought that Tyler might have made a mistake and attributed feminist tendencies to his male role. But today's women are more career-oriented, and out of necessity this can happen.

In his book, *Why Mars and Venus Collide*, Dr. John Gray writes, "The women's movement has awakened women and inspired many to find a fulfilling career in order to develop all their talents."[1] When a woman returns home from work feeling responsible for creating a beautiful home, preparing a nutritious meal, and nurturing her family, she has to do this around the demands of her job. This creates a new source of stress, and it requires a new level of support. No wonder women feel overwhelmed as they balance the demands of work and home.

Men need more support as well. Instead of coming home to rest and recover from a stressful day, a man faces a wife and family who need more from him. He attempts to provide some measure of support, but he has not had the time that he needs to recover from his daily stress. Eventually he, too, becomes tired and irritable.

The third couple, Angela and Marcus, has some issues! She talks crazy to Marcus! The worst thing a woman can do to a man is make him feel that he is worthless and unappreciated. For two-career couples, if the man is not helping out enough, the answer is to ask for his help in very specific ways rather than criticizing, rejecting, and belittling him. Even if he is tired, a project with a definite end point or solution will give him extra energy, particularly if a woman's tone of voice or facial expression while making the request indicates that she will appreciate his efforts. A man loves to please the woman he loves, and it energizes him when he knows that the woman is pleased with his actions.

Likewise most women are not automatically equipped to be the domestic, communicative, romantic partners men want. It is unrealistic for a man to expect a woman to create a beautiful home without help and appreciation, to always be in a good mood, to never be needy, and to be romantically available at all times.

Angela had to learn how to appreciate Marcus for being there in her life and supporting her efforts. Long ago she could have been giving him things to do at her beauty shop that made him feel like more of a man and a contributing partner in the relationship. Instead, she constantly reminded him that she was doing more than he was. Women have to learn how to encourage a man to feel like a man instead of castrating him.

The characters I had the hardest time accepting as reality were Sheila and Mike. As I watched the movie, I was thinking, "There is no way that any woman would let a man talk crazy to her like that. Nobody can be that mean." Our twelve-year-old son, Omari, and I were watching the movie at home and he commented, "Daddy, I couldn't be that mean if I tried."

As unbelievable as it seems, there are spouses who endure that level of abuse on a regular basis. After a while, they begin to accept the abuser's words as truth. They begin to believe they don't deserve anything more. Some women who have been both physically and verbally abused have commented that the physical abuse was easier to process. When there is physical abuse, the spouse knows she has been hit—there's an identifiable scar, there's a bruise, there's pain, there's blood. But in verbal abuse, the pain is inward and not easily identified. Therefore, it can take a while for some spouses to accept the fact that they are being abused.

Verbal and psychological abuse in a relationship can occur for a variety of reasons—the spouse's body size or composition (as in Sheila's case), intellectual ability, cooking skills, lovemaking skills, income potential, and so forth. But abuse can never solve anything. It won't motivate a spouse to lose weight. It won't help a spouse be a better lover or cook. It can't help a spouse earn more money.

It is amazing how much abuse we allow in our lives all because we have never learned how to love ourselves. That is why you must learn how to love yourself before you get married. People with high self-esteem do not tolerate abuse—not from a spouse or anyone else.

David and Michal got married for the right reason. They loved each other and wanted to be together. But something happened to separate them. When they tried to rekindle the romance, they had become different people from the two young adults who first fell in love. Because Michal had turned bitter, she became barren. Your marriage doesn't have to end like David and Michal—loveless, bitter, barren, and critical. You can decide as you are reading this book that "My marriage is going to make it!"

In the Tyler Perry movie, every year eight friends went on a trip together and made themselves look at each other and answer the question, "Why did we get married?" Are you willing to look at yourself and your spouse and answer the question? Or will you continue to blame somebody else for your unhappiness or lack of fulfillment? Now is the time to ask, "Why did I get married?" or "Why am I getting married?"

When two people enter a marriage union, there is nothing to hide. Both become vulnerable with the one that God created for him or her. In order to be vulnerable with one's spouse, there are some things that God has got to uncover in both lives so that each can return to that place of wholeness. But first, both spouses have to be willing to let Him in so He can do a perfect work in each of them and in their marriage.

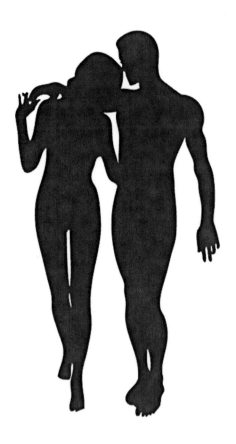

"Now to the unmarried and the widows I say: It is good for them to stay unmarried, as I am. But if they cannot control themselves, they should marry, for it is better to marry than to burn with passion."
(1 Corinthians 7:8-9)

CHAPTER FOUR
Why Do I Feel Ashamed?

The sustained deflections of Eros will sooner or later pathologize in destructive ways. It is better, then, to find a way to honor that energy than to have it enter the world in a distorted form. Thus the shadow is born, wounded Eros goes underground, and too often it breeds monsters like rape, pornography, sexual abuse of minors, and guilt-ridden acts that are at origin as much a part of one's nature as eating and sleeping. Sexuality forbidden, or constrained, is a tempting fruit, to be sure, but I am further persuaded that sex (and its accompanying fantasy of romantic love) is now carrying the burden of much of our lost spirituality. Let us acknowledge that our preoccupation with sex is putting an awesome amount of spiritual traffic across one bridge. The Shadow is not sex; but its excessive importance represents a failed treatment plan for the soul's desire for healing, for connection, for meaning. I think this is what Paul meant when he said it is better to marry than to burn.[1]

Dr. Hollis deals extensively with the "shadow self" that is part of us and that subconsciously works against us. When we do not deal with or reconcile all of who we are, the "shadow self" can play itself out in perverted ways. Such perversions have incarcerated many marriages into a cell of shame because they are afraid to reconcile all of who they are. The apostle Paul gave Christians in Corinth an outlet for their erotic side. He told them it is better to marry than it is to burn with these erotic passions. In 1 Corinthians 7:8-9 (NIV), the apostle Paul said, "Now to the unmarried and the widows I say: It is good for them to stay unmarried, as I am. But if they cannot control themselves, they should marry, for it is better to marry than to burn with passion."

Marriage ought to be a place where those passions can be fully reconciled. Marriage is the garden where couples can openly partake of the sweet fruit of marital bliss while avoiding the forbidden tree. For one reason or another, many couples are unable to enjoy any tree in the garden of marriage because they think that one bad apple has destroyed the whole garden. That apple was shame. How is shame manifested?

> O Eve, in evil hour thou didst give ear
> To that false Worm, of whomsoever taught
> To counterfeit Man's voice, true in our fall,
> False in our promised Rising; since our Eyes
> Op'nd we find indeed, and find we know
> Both Good and Evil, Good lost, and Evil got,
> Bad Fruit of Knowledge, if this be to know,
> Which leaves us naked thus, of Honour void.[2]

What happened to the good that was lost? Humanity was naked and unashamed before the serpent deceived Eve. God intended that a man and a woman brought together by His hand were to fully enjoy one another without the consciousness of their nudity. With the Fall came the knowledge of their nakedness, accompanied by their shame and feeling the need to cover up.

Before the Fall there was no need to cover up—no need to hide their true feelings, no need to hide what one spouse really desired from the other, no need to conceal deficiencies—because they were, after all, naked and not ashamed. With the Fall came an artificial cover-up with animal skins. Interestingly enough, the often publicized animal rights' group PETA (People for the Ethical Treatment of Animals) has several advertising campaigns featuring nude shots of stars protesting against wearing animal fur. The ads read, "I'd rather go naked than wear fur," or "Be comfortable in your own skin. Don't wear fur." These celebrities are making a statement that there is something unnatural about covering up with animals that have to pay the price for our vanity.

Eve, the first woman to put on fur, covered her natural beauty with animal skin because she and her husband failed to appreciate their nakedness and violated their covenant with God. Ironically, these celebs symbolize the human shift from a sacred sexuality to a secular spin on the purity of being naked and unashamed. Eve knew only her natural, God-given beauty and had no concept of the kind of manufactured beauty seen in the media. Adam didn't know that other women even existed because all of his attention was on his wife, who was uncovered for his pleasure only. They ate from the Tree of the Knowledge of Good and Evil and the consequence of their sin was information overload.

Today that tree is the media, with its many perverted branches of sensual engagement. Men, in particular, are prone to this influx of bad information. Because men are aroused by visual sensations, many find avenues to distract them from their allegiance to Eve, especially if she is covered up. A survey of U.S. adults revealed that 51 percent believe that pornography raises men's expectations of how women should look and changes their expectations of how women should behave. Beyond that, 40 percent of the adults surveyed believe that pornography harms relationships between men and women.

The Internet is an easy ticket to lustful pursuits because pornography is readily accessible. One bite from this tree can lead a man straight out of the garden of being sexually satisfied with his wife, exiting in search of the images seared into his consciousness. His pursuit forever robs them both of the innocence of a marriage inviolate.

Women and men alike must learn how to get back to where God created Adam and Eve to dwell and be. There are trees that you just don't need to eat from because the consequences complicate your marriage unnecessarily. Protecting your marriage requires knowing God's Word and knowing yourself. If you don't know God's Word, it gives the devil room to get into your head because he does know the Word.

While Jesus was in the wilderness the devil tempted Him to misuse His authority and power for selfish indulgences. He even quoted Scripture in an attempt to strengthen his case. Jesus was able to refute the devil's misuse of the Word because He knew the Word. If Jesus had yielded to the wiles of Satan, He would not have been able to break the curse of humanity's depravity caused by the fall of Adam and Eve. Jesus had to undo what the devil had done in the Garden.

The devil gave Eve some bad information. Unfortunately, she took him at his word and that led to her shame, Adam's shame, and the shame of all humanity.

Shame and Sexual Expression

Dr. Tammy Nelson, in her book, *Getting the Sex You Want*, talks about shame as it relates to the lack of sexual fulfillment. She writes, "Shame contributes to the splitting off of sexuality and erotic needs. Appreciation can go a long way to helping your partner heal from shame. Shame can keep us from feeling free and alive. Working through that shame, with the help of your partner, can free passionate energy and allow more intensity in you your erotic life."[3]

Webster's Dictionary defines shame as "a painful emotion caused by consciousness of guilt, shortcoming, or impropriety; a condition of humiliating disgrace or disrepute. Something that brings censure or reproach; something to be regretted."

Shame is a learned feeling that comes from many sources. It has its roots in our religious organizations, in our society's desire to control sexual practices and relationships, and in our own fears that we are somehow different from everyone else.

Shame, Dr. Nelson asserts, contributes to the splitting off of sexuality and erotic needs. The human need for sex and passion does not disappear if untapped; it simply splits off. It can split off into pornography, Internet relationships, extramarital affairs, sexual addiction of all kinds, and other problems. When there is no appropriate channel for our erotic needs, the energy has to go somewhere because it does not go away. That split-off energy sometimes has no outlet when there is intense shame involved.

Denise wanted to be with her husband so much. They were a committed Christian couple but ever since their baby was born, her husband didn't seem interested sexually. She longed to be touched and to be erotic with her husband again, but he would have nothing to do with her. Concealing her pent-up sexual energy, she returned to work, where Randall, one of her co-workers, often complimented her on how attractive she was. He told her how much he missed her while she was out on maternity leave and how great she looked. Every day he would find a reason to come into her office. He would always tell her how good she looked, despite her protests that she needed to get her body back in shape. As she got dressed for work each day, she began paying more attention to her appearance because she knew Randall would be watching. She took more time looking in the mirror, making sure her hair was right and that her perfume smelled good—not for her husband, but for Randall.

After a month of progressive flirting and secret lunches they had a one-night stand. By then, Denise was obviously emotionally attached to Randall, who found it awkward to work with her, knowing he only had a physical attraction to her. Over the next few weeks, she found out about a couple of other co-workers Randall had slept with. The brief interlude left Denise with nothing more than her shame. She realized she wasted something precious, something that she really wanted to give to her husband only. After Randall started giving her the cold shoulder, Denise got a reality check and put her emotions in perspective.

So many nights, Denise wanted to tell her husband that she wanted to be close to him—to be touched and held by him. She wanted him so badly.

She wanted to tell him that another man was making her feel special and it was pulling her away from him. But how do you talk to someone who may judge you for even having such thoughts, let alone acting on them?

The sexual relationship between spouses becomes difficult when there is shame. It separates one from his or her partner. One of the ways that shame happens, especially among Christian couples, is when one spouse's fantasies are imagined to be harmful to another. How can you talk to your partner about your sexual and erotic needs when you are ashamed of them? When you feel shame it can be hard to share what you really want.[4] "What fruit did you have then in the things of which you are now ashamed? For the end of those things is death" (Romans 6:21, NKJV).

The fruit of disobedience is shame. When you are in right relationship with God through Jesus Christ, you can be free of your shame. Jesus took your shame, and the shame of all humanity, upon Himself so that you can live shamelessly. There are people living in shame that no longer have to because of Jesus Christ. Even if you have violated the trust between God and your spouse it can be restored.

I Got It from Momma 'Nem!

When the apostle Paul admonished that it is better to marry than to burn with passion, he affirmed the concept that Dr. Hollis addresses about the "shadow self." The passion that human beings naturally possess, including Christians, must express itself. Instead, we try to repress it because somewhere in our lives it came out in a way that was not pleasing to God or to our little gods—namely our parents.

Parents are a child's first image of God. And in their efforts to raise their offspring to maturity, parents sometimes set unrealistic expectations as it relates to sex. The majority of the participants in the "40 Nights of Great Sex" class had never even talked to their parents about sexuality. By making the subject taboo, parents leave an empty mental chalkboard for peers, strangers, media, and the imagination to fill in. Not knowing how to reconcile all of who they are, when many couples marry, they allow the passion to manifest in negative ways or to remain penned up in shame.

When I was an adolescent, my mother helped me by giving me a book on sex, which was more like a health class explanation of what I was going through at the time. My mother, sensing my growing awareness of my sexuality, gave me the book to read to help me understand what she could not explain to me. However, it was the education I received from misguided relatives and inquisitive friends that got me on the wrong track.

Coming from a divorced family, a lot of my sexuality was discovered through trial and error—my having been introduced to sex through pornography given to me by older uncles on my thirteenth birthday, losing my virginity by age twelve—so I carried a lot of shame into my marriage. Even after my salvation and accepting my call to ministry in my junior year of college, I had to reconcile who I used to be with where God had called me to—the sacred union with my wife. To complicate matters, there was really no one in my life who could help me across the "bridge" of sexual wandering into the promised land of marital fidelity. I had to reconcile those passions and deal with my shame.

Many men and women enter marriage carrying this kind of shame because no one helped them to cross that bridge. Few parents talk to their children about sex, except to tell them "Don't do it." Unfortunately, even fewer parents model healthy sexuality by demonstrating affection for each other in front of their children. Many young adults have joked about their parents, "I know they did it at least three times, because they have three children!"

What did your parents teach you about sex? What is one word your parents might have used to describe sexuality when you were growing up? What is one word your parents would have used to describe their own sexual relationship, if you could guess? How do you think these feelings and beliefs affect you now as an adult? How do you think they affect you as a sexual being in a relationship?

"When the woman saw that the fruit of the tree was good for food and pleasing to the eye, and also desirable for gaining wisdom, she took some and ate it. She also gave some to her husband, who was with her, and he ate it. Then the eyes of both of them were opened, and they realized they were naked; so they sewed fig leaves together and made coverings for themselves" (Genesis 3:6-7, NIV). Immediately after their disobedience, Adam and Eve felt shame. They realized they were naked and tried to cover themselves. Shame comes as a result of us doing something outside the will of God; nevertheless, when we get back into right relationship with Him, we should experience our nakedness with no shame.

Eve saw that the forbidden tree was desirable for gaining wisdom (or at least that's what the serpent told her), and she saw that the fruit was good (tasty) and pleasing to the eye (alluring). She was led away to the forbidden. Adam and Eve had everything they needed there in the Garden but were deceived into eating the one thing they couldn't have.

Isn't it amazing that God gives human beings everything we need in the garden of marriage, but when we allow ourselves to be led away by our own lusts to eat from forbidden trees, we mess up our nakedness? As a result, we start covering up with inept camouflages that really don't hide who we are, because as it is mentioned in Scripture, we all are naked before God (see Hebrews 4:13). We need to discover how to get back to being naked without shame.

If you are a parent, you owe it to your children to talk to them about their sexuality at an early age. At different stages of their development you can seek material to help educate them about their bodies and what they are feeling. Children are exposed to sex earlier and earlier. When my son Jordan was eight years old, he was innocently surfing the Internet looking for Disney's *High School Musical* when a pop-up of one of the actresses nude appeared on the screen. My wife and I had to begin the sex talk earlier than planned.

We talk to our children about "good touch" and "bad touch." My wife and I show affection in front of our children. When my oldest entered junior high, we talked with him about hormones, pregnancy, STDs, and the importance of waiting until you are married to have sex with your spouse. I always tell our children that the best gift they can give their spouse one day is the gift of "them," a "them" that has not been sexually tampered with by anyone else.

In his song "Somebody's Daughter," singer Anthony Hamilton tells about how a preacher's daughter is abused at a young age and her daddy is too busy chasing the women in the church to notice that his own daughter is being molested. How profound this song is to the dilemma in today's church. While many clergy are abusing women in the church, we forget that these women are somebody's daughters. Particularly, they are the King's daughters. There are many women who still live with the scars of what happened to them when they were little girls and it shapes how they see themselves as women.

They feel shame, even though they had no control over what happened to them. Some feel shame because, even though the advances were unwanted, and they knew it was wrong, some feel shame and guilt because they did at times experience some sexual pleasure. Their responses quite often are simply a physical reaction to stimulation; nevertheless, the victim feels guilty because of those feelings.

The sexual abuse they experienced bred shame—and for many women it generates general feelings of distrust for all men, even their husbands. Many, many women who are prostitutes or who work as exotic dancers report being victims of rape or child abuse. These women enter such occupations because of their mistrust for men and refusal to experience true intimacy with them.

When Donnie McClurkin sings, his joyful voice rises from a place deep within where pain and sadness once resided. Donnie is best known for his urban anthem "We Fall Down," which topped both gospel and urban radio charts at its height. The song, with its message of forgiveness and transcendence, struck a chord with listeners worldwide—perhaps because it was such a personal testimony. The 43-year-old New York City native has had his share of obstacles that required forgiveness and overcoming.

He wrote in his 2001 autobiography, Eternal Victim/External Victor, that he was born into a family of ten siblings and an alcoholic father. As a child, he was molested by an uncle, and then raped by a male cousin when he was a teen. He credits the church with helping him heal from those experiences. Donnie moved from hurt and hate to healing and forgiveness. But unfortunately, Donnie's experience is not terribly unique. Many men, some of them husbands and fathers, are still stuck in a closet of shame from the hurt of being raped.

Donnie came out of the closet and openly talked about his rape, his confusion, his battle with homosexuality, and his deliverance from it. He worked out his own salvation, as Paul admonished us to do in Philippians 2:12. So many people choose to remain eternal victims because they are never able to talk about what happened to them.

In the movie *The Prince of Tides*, Tom Wingo (portrayed by Nick Nolte) is a man who lives with his wife and children, but has difficulty expressing intimacy. He masks his pain with sarcasm and wit. The attempted suicide of his twin sister and the news that his wife is having an affair force Wingo to examine his emotional distance and deal with a rape that happened to him as a boy. He had never told a soul. He had never discussed how it made him feel. The pain of that violated twelve-year-old boy was dominating the emotions of a forty-year-old man.

When a person is sexually violated, it plants a deep seed of shame in the soul. Outwardly, a person may appear successful, well-adjusted and happy, but inside he or she may be carrying tremendous burdens of shame—baggage. This baggage comes between a husband and wife. The intimacy they could be enjoying with one another is blocked by the baggage that keeps them from standing before each other being naked and unashamed. There are many ways for a person to be sexually violated.

Rape is forced sexual intercourse or penetration, including both psychological coercion and physical force. Forced sexual intercourse means vaginal, anal, or oral penetration by the offender(s). This category includes incidents when the penetration is from a foreign object such as a bottle. This definition includes attempted rape, male and female victims, and heterosexual and homosexual rape.

Sexual assault includes a wide range of victimizations, distinct from rape or attempted rape. These crimes include completed or attempted attacks, generally involving unwanted sexual contact between the victim and offender. Sexual assaults may or may not involve force and include such acts as grabbing or fondling. Sexual assault also includes verbal threats of a sexual nature.

Silent Victims

One of the most startling aspects of sex crimes is how many go unreported. Among the most common reasons given by victims for not reporting these crimes stem are the belief that it is a private or personal matter and that they fear reprisal from the assailant. Another reason is shame. Despite the fact that the assailant may have had a weapon, may have been physically intimidating, or was older and able to manipulate the mind of a child, victims of sexual assault often blame themselves. Their shame drives them to keep silent; thus, a terrible crime goes unreported. According to the National Crime Victimization Survey (NCVS), conducted by the U.S. Department of Justice:

- In 2001, only 39 percent of rapes and sexual assaults were reported to law enforcement officials—about one in every three.

- Of sexually abused children in grades five through twelve, 48 percent of boys and 29 percent of girls told no one about the abuse—not even a friend or sibling. [Commonwealth Fund Survey of the Health of Adolescent Girls, 1998.]

Very often, the rapist isn't a masked man or a stranger bearing candy. Often he is an acquaintance. According to the NCVS:

- Approximately 66 percent of rape victims know their assailant.

- Approximately 48 percent of victims are raped by a friend or acquaintance; 30 percent by a stranger; 16 percent by an intimate; 2 percent by another relative; and in 4 percent of cases the relationship is unknown.

These are accurate statistics. Donnie McClurkin knew his rapist and so did Tamar. The daughter of King David and the sister of Absalom, Tamar was a beautiful, young virgin, filled with so much promise—pure and beautiful. She had a beautiful multicolored coat that the king's daughters wore as a symbol that they were virgins who belonged to the king.

Can you remember the days of your innocence when you were pure? Do you remember those days when you were the apple of your daddy's eye? Do you remember when you were pure like the smell of rain after a warm day? Do you remember how innocent you were when you actually thought there was a tooth fairy? Do you remember how trusting you were when grown folks would give you candy and you didn't think anything was behind it? Do you remember your days of innocence when there was no such thing as "good touch" or "bad touch"? But perhaps somewhere along the way someone stole your innocence.

You don't have to be a woman to identify with lost innocence because there are many men who have lost their innocence. Men are not just victimizers; some are victims. We've buried it so deep that we don't want to think about it. These painful memories reside only in the darkest, deepest recesses of our minds and that is where we want to leave them.

A man deludes himself into believing that reliving those painful memories won't do any good—that talking about it won't matter. Some men don't tell because they fear that telling will emasculate them in their woman's eyes. So he lives with shame, which very often manifests as emotional detachment, even from his spouse.

The movie *Antwone Fisher* is the dramatic story of a troubled sailor who is ordered to see a naval psychiatrist about his volatile temper. With some prodding from the psychiatrist, the soldier discovers that his first step to wholeness is a remarkable emotional journey to confront his painful past—which included physical, emotional, verbal, and sexual abuse. His rage was an expression of the angry boy who was still hurting inside.

Any kind of sexual assault is painful, leaving deeply entrenched emotional scars. The pain can be even greater, however, when it comes at the hands of a family member. A young person rightfully expects family members and caregivers to be safe persons who protect and not victimize. But the testimony of many people affirms that sometimes family members are the greatest perpetrators of sexual abuse, leaving victims with mixed emotions of trust, anger, and shame.

"So Amnon lay down and pretended to be ill. When the king came to see him, Amnon said to him, 'I would like my sister Tamar to come and make some special bread in my sight, so I may eat from her hand'" (2 Samuel 13:6, NIV).

Amnon's friend told him to pretend to be sick and have the king send his sister over to him to prepare some food. When King David came to see about him, he said, "I would like my sister Tamar to come and make some special bread in my sight, so I may eat from her hand." Notice again that in this verse he called Tamar his sister; before she was Absalom's sister. Beware of people who call you brother or sister when they want something.

Some people use the words "brother" and "sister" very loosely. You need to be careful in the church that those same "brothers" and "sisters" don't turn around and violate you. When a person comes under the guise of brotherhood and sisterhood with hidden motives and agendas and takes advantage of a holy relationship, that is rape. When a brother or sister in the church comes to help you and you try to take advantage of them, that is rape. There has been a lot of rape in the church, but nobody's talking about it.

A woman once shared with me that as a teenager she was raped by her pastor. She kept the incident a secret because she didn't want to hurt her parents. When she became an adult, she finally told her parents about the terrible episode. She also found out that she was not the pastor's only victim.

"And when she had brought them unto him to eat, he took hold of her, and said unto her, Come lie with me, my sister. And she answered him, Nay, my brother, do not force me; for no such thing ought to be done in Israel: do not thou this folly. And I, whither shall I cause my shame to go?" (2 Samuel 13:11-13, KJV).

Tamar, a daughter of the king, knew that it was wrong to have sex with Amnon. She knew it would be a terrible thing to lose her virginity in that way. She tried to appeal to his sense of reason, asking, "If you do this to me where can I get rid of my shame?" Today there are still women and men in the church asking: "Where can I get rid of my shame? This happened to me by my own relative. Who can I tell?"; or, "This happened to me when I was young. I've been carrying it around all my adult life; where can I get rid of my shame?"

Many adults, particularly African Americans, have the mentality that shame is something you have to go to the grave with. They are like Miss Celie in *The Color Purple* when her daddy rapes her, impregnates her, wraps her newborn in a sheet, and tells her, "You bet' not tell nobody but God! It'd kill yo' mama." He not only took her baby, but also he stole her innocence and left shame in her womb.

Church women and men need to be liberated. Not only can you tell God, but also you can tell a counselor; you can tell your pastor. And, if a safe place has been created, you can tell your spouse. You don't have to live with that hidden shame from your childhood, no matter who it was that took your innocence.

[Tamar said,] "What about me? Where could I get rid of my disgrace? And what about you? You would be like one of the wicked fools in Israel.

Please speak to the king; he will not keep me from being married to you." But he refused to listen to her, and since he was stronger than she, he raped her. Then Amnon hated her with intense hatred. In fact, he hated her more than he had loved her. Amnon said to her, "Get up and get out!" "No!" she said to him. "Sending me away would be a greater wrong than what you have already done to me." But he refused to listen to her. He called his personal servant and said, "Get this woman out of here and bolt the door after her." So his servant put her out and bolted the door after her. She was wearing a richly ornamented robe, for this was the kind of garment the virgin daughters of the king wore. Tamar put ashes on her head and tore the ornamented robe she was wearing. She put her hand on her head and went away, weeping aloud as she went" (2 Samuel 13:13-19, NIV).

It is important for believers to expose what the devil wants to hide. That is the only way to heal it. As long as Satan can keep you entangled in secrets of shame, you continue carrying unnecessary baggage that robs you of joy and passion. People are stained by shame when they refuse to face the mess that lies within the dark corridors of their memory. Your hidden shame blocks your ability to be naked and unashamed with your spouse.

Tamar's question never got answered. After her brother raped her and put her out, she tore the multicolored coat that symbolized her virginity and put ashes on her forehead. When she told her brother Absalom, he told her to be quiet about it. She stayed with him and became a desolate woman. In other words, she kept it in the family, buried for public knowledge but not from her spirit.

Most people could never imagine the secrets that are being kept by others in closets of shame. Perhaps you are reading this knowing that you've kept quiet about your shame for too long. Maybe somebody told you to be quiet about it, to just keep it in the family, but your carrying the secret has made you a desolate woman or a desolate man. You are wasting away quietly because you don't want to embarrass your abuser, or yourself.

To hell with that! It is time to confess your hurt and your shame. The devil tries to kill you by trying to keep you quiet. The Bible states that if you confess your sins He is faithful to forgive you of all unrighteousness (see 1 John 1:9). That means not only confessing when you've sinned, but also confessing when you have been sinned against.

Our Savior said, "The truth shall make you free" (John 8:32, KJV). Gospel singer Donnie McClurkin was able to heal because he talked about what happened to him, and then he forgave his offenders. Do you want to be set free? As the old folks say, "Tell the truth and shame the devil!" You did not deserve what happened to you. Furthermore, you didn't ask for it to happen to you. Don't let the devil shame you with your secrets; shame him by confessing what happened and setting yourself free!"

Another scene I love in *The Color Purple* is when Shug Avery helps (or is it hurts?). Anyway, she gives Celie the confidence to explore her own femininity. Let me unpack this. All of her life Celie had struggled with her dark skin, her kinky hair, her mediocre features, and her low self-esteem from being verbally and sexually abused by her stepfather. Shug, who flaunts her excessive libido, mainly stemming from her father's rejection, mentors Celie in her erotic detour to lesbianism.

Celie had left an abusive stepfather only to marry the verbally and physically abusive "Mister." While watching the movie, you are left to wonder what life might have been like for Celie had she found true love from a strong Christian man who appreciated her dark skin, her natural hair, and her loving, supportive spirit. What might have happened if Mister had gently stroked her dark skin and told her as he looked into her eyes, "The darker the berry the sweeter the juice"? What if Mister had healed the wounds inflicted by her stepfather raping her and stealing her children, and loved her back to health instead of treating her as a maid, nanny, and sexual replacement for Shug Avery?

Many women struggle with a negative self-image because they have encountered too many "Misters" who have denigrated them so that their self-image is low and they don't know how to love themselves or believe that they deserve anything better. It is important for every husband to love his wife and reinforce her beauty. Beauty is truly in the eye of the beholder, but often the one that is beautiful doesn't even know it because of negative reinforcements from abusive or malicious people they have encountered.

Husbands have an obligation to speak love into the hearts of their wives. Men, remind your wife of how beautiful she is. Regardless of if she is light or dark, skinny or full-figured, has long, flowing hair or wears a weave, your wife is beautiful and you need to help her discover it before a Shug Avery does. Do not be deceived. Not only do you have to worry about "Jody" getting with your woman. Today, there is almost as great a possibility that Shug is putting the moves on her.

Regardless of their appearance, wives (and sometimes husbands too) have to get in touch with their bodies. Women are more likely than men to have body image issues, but more than a few men have been insecure about their penis size or lovemaking ability. Married couples need to move to a place in their relationship where they can make love with the lights on and the covers pulled back (both figuratively and physically). But first, they must be liberated from poor body image.

Body Image

Many men and women struggle with their body image. Because of the shame they have learned over time, they are not comfortable with their own body image. I remember a very extreme example of poor body image in Tyler Perry's movie, *Why Did I Get Married?* Jill Scott's character, Sheila, is overweight, and her verbally and emotionally abusive husband gives her constant reminders of her poor body image. In one scene, she comes into the bedroom wearing lingerie and he begins to berate her for how "stupid" she looks. Tyler takes creative license to exaggerate how some women don't feel comfortable being sexy for their husbands because of their poor body image.

Americans are obsessed with their bodies—seeking plastic surgeries, body enhancements, workout regimens, weight-loss products by the thousands—consumed with body image. If you are ashamed of your body, it makes it really hard to be naked and unashamed in your bedroom.

All of us have been programmed away from loving our bodies. We are on the constant search for a body that we may never have. We have to learn how to love the body that God has given each of us. It is vitally important that husbands and wives do not become desensitized to their own bodies. Some Christian couples need to be reintroduced to their own bodies. They have been covered up for so long that they don't even know what feels good to them. As an exercise, a married couple should lie on top of the bed covers and take turns touching every part of each other's body to see what is pleasurable and what is not. Get a chart of the body and write down on a scale of one to ten what feels the best for your spouse. If your spouse is not home, you should lie on top of the covers and touch yourself so that you can tell your spouse what feels good. Many people will be hindered from this exercise because of the shame they have been taught to feel for touching their own body.

Many women and men struggle with the "Mary the mother of Jesus versus Mary Magdalene" syndrome, referred to in Freudian psychoanalysis as the Madonna-Whore Complex. Mary, the mother of Jesus, is upheld as the ideal of what a woman should be, especially a married woman. They should be virgins and mothers. There should not be any kind of sexuality associated with them because they are mothers. They are godly wives. They are under a divine covenant with God and their husband.

On the other side of the coin, there is Mary Magdalene, a woman who had seven demons cast out of her by Jesus. Commonly believed to be a prostitute, this was a bad woman who had to be redeemed. Generally, when Christian women express their sexuality, they feel condemned to the stereotype of Mary Magdalene. In my Holy Spirit-influenced imagination I have to think that Mary Magdalene's sexuality was redeemed as well. She probably made someone a good wife because, upon her conversion, those perverted passions were channeled to her husband.

Women need to know that they can be both sexy and be saved. This has also been seen in men who have been sexually active with a woman prior to marriage, but after the nuptials, he grows sexually distant. He does not feel comfortable unleashing his manly passion on his wife or the mother of his children. Unable to find sexual fulfillment with his "madonna," he goes off to find a "Magdalene" to fulfill his needs.

We must begin by knowing that the curse has been reversed. When Jesus Christ took our place on the cross, He reversed the curse in the Garden. When Adam and Eve disobeyed God they had to leave their state of innocence, walking out of the garden with animal skins covering their nakedness. But when we look at the beginning of the redemptive act of Christ we notice that somebody leaves the Garden naked. When Jesus reversed the curse, there was an exit of a disciple who fled naked. It is deeply symbolic in the sense that Adam and Eve entered naked but left clothed. When Jesus began the redemptive work of salvation with His arrest, there was a shift from leaving the Garden clothed to now leaving naked.

"A young man, wearing nothing but a linen garment, was following Jesus. When they seized him, he fled naked, leaving his garment behind" (Mark 14:51-52, NIV; see Mark 14:44-52). This young man, who was a follower of Christ, symbolically represents us. He didn't understand why Jesus was arrested, but out of fear he ran out of the place where redemption was beginning. The guards tried to restrain him by holding on to his garments, but he left them in the Garden and ran out naked. He didn't know that he was running out naked while Jesus was taking the blame for his shame. I think many disciples are still running away from the Garden naked, not knowing that He has already taken away their shame. The young man didn't stick around to see how his salvation was worked out because of his fear and shame. He ran away naked but didn't know that Jesus took his shame.

In the Garden of Gethsemane, Jesus began the redemptive process to get rid of our shame. This young man who followed him left the Garden the opposite way that Adam and Eve did. Now some would argue that he left out of fear, and that is true. But the other truth is that Jesus did something for him that the man didn't even realize. Jesus allowed him to leave the Garden naked and unashamed.

Because of cultural, genetic, and educational misgivings, every human being carries some degree of shame. Your spouse is a helpmate who plays a vital role in helping you dispose of your shame and help make sure you enter the Garden naked and unashamed. When you have an understanding spouse who is willing to listen to you non-judgmentally, it gives you an outlet to alleviate your shame. Some people just need someone they can trust to "cover" them and not expose what they need to share or get off their chest. Many times, people are afraid to get naked because they don't know if their spouses can handle their past or their true thoughts and feelings.

For many women the ideal of marriage is interrupted by the intrusion of a third party. During our "40 Nights" workshop, a brother stood up and confessed he had brought a third party into his bedroom that had messed up his marriage. He was talking about his son. After breathing a sigh of relief, the man explained that they had a two-year-old son whom they had allowed to sleep in their bed. They had not been able to have sex because their son was always between them; baby had found a new bedroom—theirs.

Sometimes the third party is visible, like an infant child. Sometimes the third party is invisible, but even more obtrusive—like the shame brought on by poor body image, sexual secrets, a promiscuous past, secrets rooted in sexual abuse, or the politics of skin color and hair.

When either spouse is carrying concealed shame, it puts a barrier smack down in the middle of the bed. Shame creates a wide and destructive chasm in the bedroom and, therefore, in the marriage.

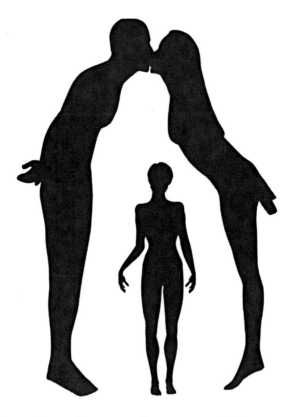

But Sarah saw the son of Hagar the Egyptian, whom she had borne to Abraham, playing with her son Isaac. So she said to Abraham, "Cast out this slave woman with her son; for the son of this slave woman shall not be heir with my son Isaac."
(Genesis 21:9-10, RSV)

CHAPTER FIVE
An Unwholesome Threesome

Since the beginning of time, a woman has always been a caretaker of life, carrying the precious seed of a life in her womb. Her body is no longer her own as she endures nine challenging months as the fetus grows inside of her womb. The mystery of giving birth, coming so close to death, and then the indescribable thrill of seeing the baby for the first time is a joy that only a mother can truly appreciate.

Then come the nights of staying up with a crying infant who can't articulate what is wrong or hovering over a feverish child. Mothering is a job like none other. As challenging as motherhood is, even under the best of circumstances, many women have the added pressure of raising a child or children on their own. It is one thing to have to get up with a baby at three o'clock in the morning and have a husband to trade off with you, as opposed to getting up at 3:00 a.m. and then getting dressed for work at 6:00 a.m. because you are both nurturer and provider.

It is one thing to have a planned pregnancy and a spouse to share the joy of the baby's arrival. It is altogether different when you are not planning to get pregnant and the one who planted the seed does not welcome the news, leaving you alone on the journey of parenthood.

Whether you are a devoted mother and wife or a single mother with a reluctant father, this chapter goes out to all the baby's mamas, because none of us would have life had it not been for you. I think rapper The Game summarizes it best in "Hate It or Love It." He said that whenever he feels exhausted, like he wants to give up, he thinks about the fact that his mother chose not to have an abortion. Mamas, we're all glad that you didn't give up, even when the choice was difficult.

Believe it or not, every mother's story was not one of a planned pregnancy with a supportive husband. For some women, the news of pregnancy brought both tears and fears because of the timing or the circumstances. The father may have been married to someone else. He may have been a one-night stand. The father may have been a side affair—not her real man.

Realizing that many of the women reading this book will fall into one of those categories, I do not want to disrespect your dignity or the nobility of who you are. However, I do want to show some love for the women who didn't enter into motherhood gracefully, but who, once there, worked the hand that was dealt to them.

The story of Abraham, Sarah, and Hagar is indicative of the whole human struggle as it relates to the mothering process of today. It is the story of a pregnancy amid inconvenient circumstances, as often still happens today. The ideal picture of family is a man and woman who have a promise from God that He will make them fruitful and multiply. But He never tells us that things don't always work according to our timetable and that what looks like a denial is really only a delay. It is how we respond to the delay that sometimes gets us in trouble.

The Danger of Threesomes

When God promised Abraham and Sarah that He would make a nation from their offspring, it was hard for Sarah to accept it because she was already well beyond her childbearing years. By the time God spoke to them, she was an old woman who had already been through menopause. In an effort to "help God out," she took matters into her own hands and told her husband to have sex with their young, fertile slave girl.

It is when we take matters into our own hands that we begin to make matters worse instead of better. It is when we try to speed up God's plan that we get ourselves in a mess. Paradise is disturbed in many marriages because the couple gets to a point when they feel they need to devise a plan to fix what ain't working. But they don't go about it God's way. Bringing a third party into your marriage bed is a quick way to defile what God has ordained and a certain road to disaster. Sarah's bright idea of bringing in a third party into their marriage was something she would regret later.

It may seem totally inappropriate to be discussing "threesomes" from a Christian perspective, but we are living in a time when it is necessary. One day I got a telephone call from a friend of mine who is a minister of music at a large church. I told him that I was writing to help strengthen Christian marriages in their sexuality. He asked me if I was going to discuss "threesomes." When I wondered why, he told me that one of his choir members was approached by a very professional man whom he had seen many times at the gym with his wife. The man said, "My wife and I have been checking you out and she is very attracted to you. Would you mind having sex with my wife?"

He then told me that another couple in the church had invited a lesbian into their bedroom. The wife became emotionally attached to the lesbian and left her husband for the woman.

With TV shows like *Swingtown* airing on CBS, there is a need to discuss the consequences of third parties involved in our sex lives. Swingers are couples, usually in committed relationships, who like to have sex with another party or other couples. In the sex-crazy, free-love 1970s, the era in which *Swingtown* is based, threesomes were easy to achieve, but even secular sex self-help books warn couples of the consequences of threesomes: "Swinging comes with a hefty 'try at your own risk' warning: Most end up feeling jealous, and in lots of cases, motivation is lopsided. One partner wants to try it; the other goes along with it for fear of losing them if they don't. It can and does lead to split-ups," according to Tracy Cox, author of *Superhotsex* (DK Adult, 2006). Christians must understand that having third-party sex is not only forbidden in Scripture, it is just too dangerous emotionally, and sometimes physically as well.

Sarah and Abraham's decision turned out to be dangerous, with emotional and physical ramifications. It was legal for Sarah to give her slave girl to her husband, but it wasn't beneficial. "'Everything is permissible for me'—but not everything is beneficial. 'Everything is permissible for me'—but I will not be mastered by anything'" (1 Corinthians 6:12, NIV). There are many things that you can do that are legal, but they are not beneficial. It is true that you are grown and can do what you want, but you have to ask yourself before you get into something disastrous, "Is this the best for me in the long run?"

Hagar could not protest the arrangement because she was a slave, but you are not like Hagar. You can say "no" to any bad situation and avoid a lot of mess because you are no longer a slave. Whom the son sets free is free indeed (see John 8:36). You don't have to settle for an extramarital relationship with married men—you are free. You don't have to be part of a love triangle—you are free. You don't have to be with a married man who only wants you because his wife can't perform sexually—you are free! You don't sabotage your marriage by bringing in a third-party, extramarital affair. You are free from the pornography that you thought could bring satisfaction to your sex life with your spouse.

Of course, Hagar complied with Sarah's wishes, and conceived a child by Abraham. That is when the real trouble began. According to Genesis 16, Sarah took her Egyptian maidservant and gave her to Abraham. As her body underwent the changes of pregnancy, it affected her emotions. She became irritable and resentful of Sarah. What was once an orderly and healthy relationship became an entangled mess. When Hagar became pregnant, she tried to maintain some pride and dignity and make the most of a bad situation. But her mistress Sarah didn't appreciate the way Hagar got beside herself. Sarah went back to Abraham and blamed him for their being in the predicament. She got Abraham's permission to beat Hagar down. When Hagar retreated into the wilderness to escape Sarah's harsh treatment, an angel met her there and asked, "Hagar, servant of Sarai (Sarah), where have you come from, and where are you going?" (Genesis 16:8, NIV).

The angel instructed Hagar to return to her mistress, and she complied. Further, God promised to make a nation out of her and her son as well. Then, seventeen years later, when it was about time for Ishmael to get his inheritance, Sarah looked outside and saw that Ishmael was taunting his three-year-old brother Isaac. She didn't like what she saw: Hagar's teen-aged son was teasing her three-year-old baby, Isaac. She remembered that Ishmael soon would be eighteen and, as the oldest son, was rightfully heir to his father's inheritance. But she knew that her child was the son God had promised to her and Abraham.

Sarah told Abraham to send his son Ishmael away because he had no share in the inheritance of our son Isaac. This lifelong conflict still goes on today. What happens to the babies that are born outside the promise of the marriage covenant? In biblical times, there was a law that protected the children of slave women, but it did not guarantee them an inheritance. What happens to Hagar's child when he threatens the inheritance of Sarah's child? What happens when you are the other woman, whether by choice or by circumstance, and your children are put in a precarious situation?

God told Abraham that he had to separate his spiritual child from his fleshly child. Abraham loved them both but he had to make a distinction between the child he had outside of marriage and the child he had with his wife. Abraham struggled with this decision; however, some men would put Hagar and her son away without even thinking about it or they wouldn't even tell Sarah about Ishmael at all. In the movie Look Who's Talking, Mollie is a single, professional woman who gets pregnant by her married lover, Albert. In her heart she hoped he would step up and do what was right by her and the baby. What she found out was that he was really only concerned about himself. Albert cared about the needs of his children by his wife, but he never really showed interest in the needs of Mollie's son, Mikey.

Men can be like that. Many show little concern for the welfare of children born outside the marriage relationship. And when they pay the mother child support, often it is just a check coming every month— not a father to love, protect, and guide the child into adulthood. Abraham struggled with the welfare of his son born outside of his marriage. But God told Abraham "Don't be distressed. I'm getting ready to clean up what you messed up. Don't worry about Ishmael. I will take care of him and his mother because, like I told you, the inheritance belongs to the child of the covenant. But I also have made provisions for the child you brought into this world on your own."

So with the Lord's assurance, Abraham gave Ishmael and Hagar a skin of water and some bread and put them on the bus. Their bus fare only took them out into the desert, and with no connections. I know Hagar was hurting when she saw what Abraham was giving her. She probably felt like Fantasia when she sang, "I see you get that support check in the mail. You open it and you're like 'What the Hell?'" Their food ran out in a matter of days. Their water also ran out and Hagar and her teenaged son were dehydrated and stuck in the desert.

Thank God for all of the mothers who love their children and look out for them. Hagar was in the desert with no food and no child support, and she ran out of water. Like so many single mothers throughout the generations, she tried to make the best out of a bad situation.

There are many Hagars out there today. You knew that the relationship wasn't healthy but you couldn't deny the baby that came out of it. Still, you find yourself stuck in the desert with no food and your baby is dehydrated. Maybe it is not physical dehydration; maybe he is dying from father hunger. Maybe what is really killing him is that his daddy doesn't accept him. Maybe what is killing your daughter is that she can't get any love from Daddy and she can't get any from you either, because you are always working, trying to take care of her. You are trying to have some dignity in being a single mother, but it is hard when all you have is some bread and a skin of water, and what little you had just ran out.

Hagar had to sit her son under a tree while she went over a stone's throw away so she wouldn't have to watch him die. Some mothers become emotionally distant from their children because they don't want to see them die. These mothers go in the next room to cry at night because they don't know how they are going to make provisions for their children. They don't say much to their children because they don't know how to raise boys into men by themselves. They are at work, but they can't concentrate because they are wondering what they are going to fix for dinner when the cupboard is bare.

If you're a single mother, you've probably had times when there was more month than money. Everybody knows that the baby you had didn't come from being inside the marriage covenant, but you love your child and you know it is not her fault for being born into this situation. You didn't want it to happen like this, but the reality is that she is here and her daddy isn't. You're left to wonder, "Lord, what am I supposed to do now? I don't have the support. I don't have the money. It looks like we're going to die."

Hagar thought they were going to die. But "God heard the boy crying, and the angel of God called to Hagar from heaven and said to her, 'What is the matter, Hagar? Do not be afraid; God has heard the boy crying as he lies there. Lift the boy up and take him by the hand, for I will make him into a great nation.' Then God opened her eyes and she saw a well of water. So she went and filled the skin with water and gave the boy a drink" (Genesis 21:17-19, NIV).

Have you been or are you currently caught up in a love triangle? If you are, everything you need to get out of it is right under your nose. You may have been trying to go dig up something when what you need already has been dug up for you. There is a well of resources found in the story of Abraham, Sarah, Hagar, Ishmael and Isaac.

Ladies, you don't have to settle for Abraham—somebody else's man—when God has a man just for you.

Men, you don't have to play the role of Abraham—torn between the needs of two women, of two children, and trying to keep the peace.

The plight of single sisters today seems insurmountable, with the shortage of available men, especially in the black community. As we move toward the ideal of every Eve being married to her Adam, the plight of single women must be addressed as a critical part of getting back to the Garden.

*Behold, the wicked man
conceives evil, and is
pregnant with mischief,
and brings forth lies.
(Psalm 7:14, RSV)*

CHAPTER SIX
Who Got You Pregnant?

Tim Harford, author of *The Logic of Life*, wrote in an article on the plight of single mothers: "There are a lot of African-American single moms around and some commentators are inclined to blame this fact on 'Black Culture." Harford's latest exploration, the rational behaviors of black women when large numbers of black men are "unmarriable," has caused quite a stir. For policy makers and society in general—all of whom are indoctrinated to believe that black out-of-wedlock births, low marriage rates, single-parent households, and all the attendant societal ills are a result of a lack of morals entrenched in black culture—Harford offers a logical explanation. "Marriage markets" where there are large numbers of black men in prison significantly reduce the lifetime chances of marriage among black women. In other words, the relationship choices of many black women have less to do with morals and more to do with survival.

Harford writes, "Whom you marry depends on where you live, but also on how old you are and what race you are. Most people marry people of the same race, of a similar age and from the same area: 96 percent of married Black women have Black husbands and over 96 percent of married white women have white husbands." Since large numbers of black women have not yet expanded their pool of prospective husbands beyond the black community, the shortage of available men due to incarceration logically leads to many women remaining single.

A recent report from the Pew Center on the States announced the U.S. now has the largest number of prisoners ever—2.3 million—and half are black men. That is an extreme case, but there are thirty-two states with more than one-in-ten young black men in prison, and ten states where one-in-six young black men are behind bars. According to Harford, "That is serious business for young Black women."

These are desperate times for sisters who find themselves still single with few options for marriage. What do you do when it seems that your choice of available men is limited and your biological clock is ticking? Sometimes women place themselves in compromising positions when desperation sets in. I don't think it is our culture that causes women to be single mothers, but, rather, the conditions that create the likelihood for many black women to be without husbands and fathers for their children. What happened to the men who fathered these children but are not around to raise them? If the pool to pick a father was shallow, then I need to ask, "Who got you pregnant?"

Tamar was a sister desperately trying to conceive. She had married Judah's son Er, whose name means "awake." He was the first man in Tamar's life. Through Tamar's marriage to Er, she was awakened to the possibility that she would have a family. She awakened to the possibility of a solid and secure future with a man, a son of Judah. However, she was never able to conceive with this man because he was an evil man. Er died before they could conceive a child.

Pregnancy, in those days, was a woman's badge of honor. If a woman was not able to give birth it became a badge of shame and was deemed to be punishment from God. The woman's God-given purpose, so they believed, was that she would be the vessel to carry on the family name. Therefore, every woman wanted to give her husband a son to carry on the family name. Every woman wanted to get married and be fruitful for her husband. But it looked like it would never happen for Tamar because her husband had died too soon.

For a lot of women reading this book, something died in your first relationship. You had high hopes that this would be the man that you would have children with. This first man was the man you really loved. You thought that love was awakened, and when you opened up to him, you thought that he would be in your life forever. Instead, something died and it left you barren, broken, and by yourself. You wondered if you would ever bounce back from this disappointment.

Margaret Mead, the famous anthropologist, said we have three marriages in our lifetime. The first is for children, the second is for sex, and the third is for companionship. Tamar married the first time for children. This is what a woman does. She hooks up with a man because of her cultural obligation to find a mate that she hopes will be with her forever and give her some children. But somewhere in the second relationship, you get stuck with a man who simply wants you for sex but doesn't want you for marriage.

Judah gave Tamar his second son, Onan. He was supposed to help Tamar retain her dignity by marrying her to give her a son to carry on the family name. It was an ancient custom that upon the death of a husband, the brother-in-law would then impregnate the widow to carry on his brother's name. The problem was that Tamar didn't know that he had married her for sex and not for children. The Bible says that whenever he would lay with her, instead of allowing his seed to impregnate her, he would withdraw and spill his seed on the ground. Too much is wasted when we allow ourselves to get into relationships that are nothing more than sexual recreation. You are wasting seed.

Sex was created for a husband and a wife to procreate more so than recreate. There is nothing wrong with recreational sex within a healthy married relationship, but many women never get to this point because the man they are with is not connected to them emotionally. They are having sex on two different levels. Onan repeatedly used the law that would have provided for his brother's lineage for his own selfish sexual gratification. He took advantage of the situation, but refused the responsibility that went with it. So God took his life too (see Genesis 38:10). Not only does indiscriminant sex waste your seed physically, but also financially.

There is a responsibility that comes along with sex, whether within marriage or outside of it. You cannot just have sex for personal gratification without owning up to your responsibility. When a man lays down with a woman, he must ask himself, "Am I willing to be responsible as a husband for this woman I'm about to lay down with?" If you can't be responsible for your seed, then you shouldn't be lying down with any woman.

Men, if you are not willing to be that woman's husband and give her children, you shouldn't be wasting your seed. God will take you out for wasting your seed. AIDS is a reminder that God doesn't like us wasting our seed. God created a union between a man and a woman whereby they could plant seeds in holy matrimony and enjoy the planting process. Unfortunately, many people have gotten into relationships that are wasteful because they have been deceived into unions that promised procreation; but in reality it was only for recreation.

Onan's behavior toward Tamar mirrors Harford's theory that posits black men who see that they are only competition behind bars, thus they have no incentive to marry. The sex imbalance caused by imprisonment allows black men who are not in jail to enjoy themselves sexually without the commitment or responsibilities of marriage. So they don't. Even though they could, it appears that young black men who are not in prison typically take advantage of their strong bargaining position by not bothering to marry at all. Thus there are a lot of Tamars who are in relationships with Onans but are not married to them. These brothers know Tamar's desperation and use it to their advantage, often sexually as well as financially. They have no intention of marrying her, or fulfilling the marital duty because they are only in it for the sex.

After Onan died, there was only one son left to Judah. He told Tamar that when Shelah got older, he would give her his last son to continue the family name. And even though Judah promised to give his youngest and only living son to Tamar, he secretly feared that he would befall the same fate as his brothers. Tamar was a young widow with plenty of potential, single with the promise that when this boy matured he would marry her. Tamar seems to be the picture of a lot of single sisters today. They have been in love relationships where they lost their mate to his own self-destructive ways. Then, they wind up in relationships that seem centered around somebody else getting pleasure from their pain. When they get out of that relationship, they spend more time waiting for some boy to turn into a man—waiting for a man to fulfill his promise, knowing deep down that it's never going to happen.

What is a woman to do when she has already been let down twice and it looks like her biological clock is winding down? What do you do when all your relatives are looking at you and saying, "Girl, what are you waiting for? When are you going to have a baby?" What do you do when you married for children, married for sex, and now you just want somebody to love you?

I believe that some of you reading this are Tamar readers who have just been looking for what rightfully belongs to you. You've been looking for dignity in the marriage bed, but it seems that drastic times call for drastic measures. You never thought that you would have done some of the things you've done now. If you are desperate for love and fulfillment, you may become vulnerable enough to compromise your values just to have even a semblance of happiness. When it seems that time is running out, you may even allow yourself to forfeit your dignity in exchange for quick fixes that really end up becoming long-term problems. Tamar resorted to drastic, unscrupulous methods to get pregnant, trying to take away the shame of what was done to her. But in reality, she only shamed herself further by trying to avoid shame.

You may feel this same sense of desperation. But remember, you are not the one who put your man in jail. You are not the one who got him killed in a senseless act of violence. You wanted more than just recreational sex.

You took what was given to you but you were left standing with nothing but shame. You never asked that the ratio between men and women would increase. By the time blacks reach their late twenties, there are 128 black women for every one hundred black men.

Keisha is only twenty-two years old, but she has spent the last eight years desperately looking for love in all the wrong places. Her penchant for "thug boys" caused her to pick males she found "exciting." Her first pregnancy occurred at age fifteen. Shortly after her son was born, his father went to prison, so she was left to raise the boy with little support from her family or that of the father. A couple of years later, she met another guy and soon became pregnant again. This time, she married the baby's father, but the responsibility of a wife and two children proved too much for her twenty-year-old husband and he bailed. Separated but never divorced, Keisha found another guy she thought would give her the love and the family life she claimed to want so badly. He impregnated her and has spent most of his time in and out of jail since their baby was born.

Today, Keisha is overwhelmed with the responsibility of three young children and no stable means of support. Once having high hopes and dreams of earning a college degree, she has allowed her desperation to lead her to the wrong kind of man time and time again. Consequently, she has ended up a college dropout with three children fathered by three different men, but never a real man in her life.

Asking, "Why do Blacks have more concurrent sexual encounters?", Cunningham (http://www.slate.com/id/2182089/entry/2182090) found the relative shortage of men may cause women to feel desperate about the prospects of finding a stable partner, encouraging short-term relationships with less-committed mates. This may explain the motivation of attractive black women fighting over sorry, useless men on the shows like Jerry Springer and Flavor of Love.

Tamar was desperate. So desperate that she felt she had to deceive in order to conceive. She abandoned her morals and her principles in order to do what she thought she had to do to preserve her dignity. She decided to dress up as a prostitute to get pregnant by her father-in-law. That's desperate. Isn't it amazing that in order to preserve her dignity she did something deceptive? In her mind she thought this was the only way she could get what she thought she needed by having a baby. So many sisters get desperate and think, "If I have a baby, then maybe this will give me the dignity I've been looking for." But you don't have to prostitute yourself to get the dignity you deserve. Prostituting yourself doesn't elevate dignity; it destroys dignity and pummels self-esteem.

A woman on a mission, In Genesis 38, Tamar disguised herself as a prostitute, put a veil over her face and went out of town to where Judah was. Thinking she was indeed a prostitute, Judah saw her and asked her to sleep with him. She asked him what would she receive in return for her sexual favors. Judah replied, "I will send you a young goat." Untrusting because of her previous disappointments and hurt dealing with men, she holds out for a guarantee that Judah will keep his word. She asked him, "What are you going to give me to make sure you will give me what you said?" He gave her his seal, cord, and staff. Then, the Bible says, she lay down with him and became pregnant.

The Bible reminds us that when we are pregnant with evil and conceive, trouble gives birth to disillusionment (Psalm 7). Tamar had to deceive in order to get what she thought she needed. The penalty for a woman prostituting and getting pregnant out-of-wedlock was death.

Somebody came to Judah and said, "Your daughter-in-law has been prostituting and is pregnant."

He said, "Bring her out here so we can burn her." Tamar had been exposed for her misdeeds and was about to burned alive her along with her baby.

But as they were pulling her out of the house she said, "Wait a minute! Before you throw me in the fire, take this seal, this cord, and this staff and tell Judah that these items belong to my baby's daddy."

Judah realized that the prostitute he thought he slept with was really his daughter-in-law, Tamar. Judah recognized her and said, "She is more righteous than I, since I wouldn't give her to my son Shelah." And he did not sleep with her again.

The only thing that saved Tamar was that she was pregnant by Judah, whose name meant "praise." She was pregnant with Praise's baby. Even in the midst of her manipulation, God spared her life and gave her twin sons because she was pregnant by Praise. For all the Tamars reading this, whether you are male or female, you need to know that nobody can judge you because of how you felt you had to survive. We all have had times in our lives—times when we went low to get high.

You are not the only one who has wasted your seed. You are not the only one who has deceived somebody simply trying to get love. But if you are going to survive the trouble you are in, you'd better make sure you are pregnant with praise. No matter if you played the prostitute, played the harlot, played the whoremonger, or have been in an abusive relationship, you can decide that no matter what, "I'm going through! I'm going to make sure I'm pregnant with praise because the Bible says that when praises go up blessings come down."

That is the irony of God. Even in the midst of turmoil and deception, God can still come in. "But where sin abounded, grace did much more abound" (Romans 5:20, KJV). When you are a sister or a brother trying to survive during desperate times, there are four things you need to do.

1. Be careful how you conceive. What you give birth to starts with conception.

2. Plan your pregnancy. Determine that you will give yourself to somebody who's going to handle his or her marriage responsibilities.

3. Don't prostitute yourself. You shouldn't have to cheapen who you are to achieve the desires of your heart.

4. Remember, God gives the blessing. God is able to give birth to your breakthrough.

When the time came for her to give birth, there were twin boys in her womb. As she was giving birth, one of them put out his hand; so the midwife took a scarlet thread and tied it on his wrist and said, "This one came out first." But when he drew back his hand, his brother came out, and she said, "So this is how you have broken out!" The second brother was named Perez. Then the brother who had the scarlet thread on his wrist, came out and he was given the name Zerah.

When Tamar gave birth to twin boys, Zerah (scarlet) began to come out first and they tied a scarlet ribbon around his wrist. It is stated in Isaiah 1:18 (NIV), "Though your sins are like scarlet, they shall be as white as snow." It looked like she had conceived sin, but then the other son jumped out in front of him. His name, Perez, means "breakthrough." God has a way of giving you breakthrough in spite of your sin!

What you have been through should have killed you, but because you were pregnant with praise God withdrew your sin and gave you a breakthrough. Once God gives you breakthrough in spite of your sin, you need to focus on your relationship with the spouse that God has given you. When God finally blesses you with your soulmate, and the two of you are on the same page sexually, you need to understand that there still will be tension. There will be times, even in paradise, when you will not agree.

Marriage is not always the Garden of Eden it is supposed to be. We often idealize marriage as a conflict-free state between a man and a woman, but the reality is that a good marriage has healthy conflict. My wife and I were talking one day about those times when we are at odds due to an unpleasant disagreement. I told her as iron sharpens iron, so one spouse sharpens the other! The reality is that when those sparks fly, it is only because they are needed to strengthen the relationship. Let's go into the next chapter so we can see how to solve the conflict or tension between husband and wife.

*But the Lᴏʀᴅ God called
to the man, "Where are you?"
He answered, "I heard you
in the garden, and I was afraid
because I was naked; so I hid."
(Genesis 3:9-10, NIV)*

CHAPTER SEVEN
Tension Between Adam and Eve

"And he said, 'Who told you that you were naked? Have you eaten from the tree that I commanded you not to eat from?' The man said, 'The woman you put here with me—she gave me some fruit from the tree, and I ate it'" (Genesis 3:11-12, NIV).

The Fall created a new reality of woundedness between men and women. After the Fall, life between the sexes became cursed and infected with personal agendas and power plays. Look at God's words to Eve in Genesis 3:16 (NASB): "In pain you will bring forth children; Yet your desire will be for your husband, And he will rule over you."

Robert Lewis brings out an interesting point in his book, *The New Eve*. He says as a result of the Fall, husband and wives are at odds because of the curse of Adam and Eve. The woman was supposed to be a helper to the man and the man was supposed to be in harmony with the woman. As a result of the Fall, however, the woman is lost in a power struggle with the man, constantly feeling a pull in her spirit as to whether she should submit to her husband or remain independent. Look at his comparison of the word desire.

Desire is clearly associated with the idea of control. God told Cain that sin sought to control him. That was its aim. And this understanding of desire helps us unlock Genesis 3:16. The woman's desire in Genesis 3:16 is also the desire to control in Genesis 7:7. The consequences of the Fall will taint even a woman's true love for her husband into an unholy struggle. From this point on, a woman's calling as helper will be mixed with the desires of a competitor.[1]

The husband and wife's intimacy is threatened by the war of wills. This war can be seen so often in marriages where there is a "war of the roses" instead of a celebration of what ought to be sweet communion. Men long to be in communion with their wives, but instead seem to be in constant tension and can't understand the pull. It is a spiritual war that takes place between a man and a woman and sets up what seems to be a constant pull between the two. There are differences between the man and woman that can be overcome if we are willing to look deeper into what distinguishes Adam from Eve.

God Told Eve

Here is what God said to Eve (Genesis 3:16, NIV):

"I will greatly increase your pains in childbearing; with pain you will give birth to children. Your desire will be for your husband, and he will rule over you" (Genesis 3:16, NIV).

1. You will have pain in childbearing.

Women endure great sacrifice when bearing children. One of the things that sometimes separates Adam from Eve is the children that Eve bears. It has been said that the libido of a woman can sometimes be low because the oxytocin levels go down when the woman is nursing. Further, the responsibility of raising children usually falls disproportionately with the mother. After a day filled with caring for children, or sometimes working themselves and then coming home to raise children, most men still expect that their wives should always be willing and ready to have sex. A man may not take into account that his wife may be tired from birthing and raising his children—sometimes working a full-time job in addition.

2. Your desire will be for your husband.

At first glance, this sounds like good news for the man, but with Robert Lewis's interpretation of desire, meaning "control," it is not such good news. Sometimes a woman's need to talk to her husband can seem like control, but actually her talk reflects her desire to be heard. It can seem like control because men are not wired to listen to great detail, particularly as it is repeated over and over again. Men are fixers. We want to solve the problem and move on. Women don't necessarily want their problem solved when they talk about it. They want to be heard and to be cared for. A woman's desire is for her husband to listen to her lovingly, with compassion and understanding.

3. He will rule over you.

Because of the Fall, there will always be this feeling among wives that their husbands are trying to make them into something they are not. Conversely, men feel like they need to conquer, and sometimes their nearest competitor seems to be their wives. So, a man's dilemma becomes, How do I get the sex I want, the love I want, without demanding it from my wife?

God Told Adam

Here is what God said to Adam (Genesis 3:17-19, NIV):

> "Because you listened to your wife and ate from the tree about which I commanded you, 'You must not eat of it,' 'Cursed is the ground because of you; through painful toil you will eat of it all the days of your life. It will produce thorns and thistles for you, and you will eat the plants of the field. By the sweat of your brow you will eat your food until you return to the ground, since from it you were taken; for dust you are and to dust you will return.'"

1. Because you listened to your wife...

Because Adam took bad advice from his wife, the tendency of a man is to second-guess what his wife is saying. Ironically, though many women are more discerning than men, often a husband will refuse to heed his wife's advice because something in him distrusts what she says. Men have to learn to listen again because the Fall took away our hearing and our trust of our helpmate.

2. By the sweat of your brow you will eat your food.

Men are workers. Sometimes men get consumed in their work to the point that they forget about family. Family often gets a man's leftovers and then he doesn't understand why he can't get the love he wants from his wife after he comes in tired. The reality is, she's just as tired as he is.

3. It will produce thorns and thistles for you.

Working can cause men pain to the point that they become desensitized to touch. Their outer persona can become calloused because of the exposure to the elements and, therefore, they forget how to be sensitive and romantic when they are off the clock.

Bridging the Gender Gap

Many couples yearn to return to the blissful state of "oneness" but they just don't know how to overcome the gap of non-existing communication. For whatever reason, they are not communicating like they used to. The enemy came in and disrupted the connection between two people who once seemed inseparable. What can Adam and Eve do to bridge the gap between them? There are many things that both Adam and Eve can do to repair the breach by counteracting the curse of poor communication.

What Can Adam Do?

Adam can relearn the art of listening. There is a difference between listening and hearing. Many husbands have learned the art of pretending to listen but really they haven't heard a word their wives have said. Listening and hearing involves a husband giving his wife undivided attention and repeating back to her what he has heard her saying. Adam's sin wasn't that he listened to his wife; his mistake is that he didn't use his good judgment as leader to listen then respond back to what he understood as right. As we will explore later in the Imago Dialogue, there is a way for husbands and wives to listen to each other, but it doesn't mean that they have to agree to everything that the other wants to do.

Adam can also learn how to help the woman with the job of rearing the children. For the most part, in this post-modern era the roles of both husband and wife are blurred. Gone are the days when Mr. Cleaver leaves for work, leaving Mrs. Cleaver in the kitchen washing dishes wearing a dress and heels, and sporting a pearl necklace. Today's husbands don't return home to find that sons Beaver and Wally are sitting at the dinner table waiting on him so they can all eat dinner together.

Today, there usually are two breadwinners in the home. Today's women work just as hard as men. Therefore, effectively taking care of home needs the teamwork of both husband and wife. A man has a tendency to want to come home, kick off his shoes, pick up the remote and unplug until dinner is ready. This is the way he de-stresses. Then, when he comes out of his cave, he expects his wife to be willing and ready for an exciting evening of sexual passion.

In order for a man to get the sex and intimacy he desires, he must become willing to make the sacrifice of taking more time to help raise his children, which includes things like feeding them and putting them to bed. When his wife sees that he is willing to help her around the house, it lowers her stress level and makes her oxytocin levels raise. Oxytocin is the chemical in women that causes them to feel loved and aroused. When a man sees his woman turned on and smiling, it causes his own testosterone levels to go up. Testosterone is a chemical in men that contributes to their sexual arousal. Both Adam and Eve forget about how tired they are when this chemical reaction between oxytocin and testosterone takes place.

Dr. John Gray has written an excellent book on the differences between men and women and how it affects their sexual lives. In *Mars and Venus in the Bedroom*, Gray asserts that one of the requirements for great sex is that women not feel pressured to perform in any way. Men tend to be performance-driven. A man feels successful when he gives his wife pleasure. But if he feels that he has to score a touchdown (an orgasm for the woman) every time, then he unknowingly can put undue pressure on his wife. His actions can be perceived as controlling when all he is really trying to do is give to his wife and please her.

One mistake men make is that when a man discovers something that gives pleasure to his wife, he tends to wear that one "thing" out! For example, if his wife is pleased by oral sex, a man will tend to go straight for the "end zone" instead of spending time exploring the rest of her body. His focusing only on that one area leaves his wife feeling like she has no say in her own pleasure. But in the man's mind, he has discovered what works and he wants to keep doing it right.

What Can Eve Do?

Give him time to rest from the field. Because men and women are wired differently, we de-stress differently. Women need to talk to de-stress while men need to unplug to de-stress.[1] One of the best gifts that Eve can give her husband is time to unplug from his day. When he comes home from work, give him something to drink and let him retreat to his cave for a while. When he has an opportunity to go into his decompression chamber, after he comes out he will be more of a gift to her and to the family. It is like an astronaut who travels to outer space. The astronaut has come into contact with all kinds of toxic elements in outer space and has been without oxygen, gravity, etc. He or she must go through decompression before reentering the earth's atmosphere. Men must be allowed to go through their own decompression rituals of doing "right" brain activities so they can forget about the pressures in the left brain. Give Adam some rest.

Trust your husband's leadership. There is an ongoing struggle with men trying to prove to their wives that they really have the best interest of their families at heart. Author Bunny Wilson has said that women are liberated through submission. There is something wonderfully peaceful that happens when a woman decides to trust the leadership of her husband and surrenders to the will of God.

Once while counseling a couple I asked the wife who was the head of their house. She replied rather defiantly, "God!" Then after about thirty seconds of pensive stares, she reluctantly conceded, "and my husband." Men have to fight many battles out in the world trying to provide for their families. There is one fight that he doesn't want to engage in when he gets home, and that is with his wife.

Reintroduce him to touch. Men have been conditioned through time to be tough because of their exposure to the elements. A woman's skin is ten times more sensitive than a man's skin. Men need to be reintroduced to touch. The challenge is that men are more able to feel only after they have had sex. Before a woman can get a man to feel her, he has to be stimulated. A woman needs a lover with a slow hand, but a man needs his woman to run directly for the border.

It is as though all of the man's nerve endings are in one place—his penis. When a woman stimulates a man there, it opens his sensitivities to touch on the rest of his body.

Give him some. Women need to be heard in order for them to feel affection and then arousal. Men need to have sex before they can open up emotionally. As a man's heart opens during orgasm, he is able to feel the depth of his love and reaffirm his commitment to his wife, according to *Mars and Venus in the Bedroom.*[2]

One of the most dangerous tools of the devil is emotional distance. That is why Paul urged married couples not to abstain from sex for a long period or else the enemy would come in. It is interesting that when the serpent comes to tempt Eve, Adam is not mentioned. It can be assumed that either he was not there or he was not vocal if he was there. Either way the enemy came in and manipulated the understanding to what Eve knew as right and wrong.

Emotional distance occurs when husbands and wives stop communicating with one another. Emotional distance between the man and the woman will always cause the enemy to come in and manipulate what they know to be right and wrong. Emotional distance can be caused by at least ten factors:

1. Unfaithfulness
2. Arguments
3. Grudges
4. Busyness
5. Depression
6. Low sex drive in one spouse
7. Lack of spiritual intimacy
8. Lack of romance
9. Rejection
10. Not asking for what you want

Unfaithfulness

When one spouse steps outside of the marriage covenant and commits adultery, it causes a rift between the man and the woman. Before the affair is even discovered the fracture is already there. Like a hairline fracture in the leg of an athlete, the splinter and the pain will only get worse, especially the more it is used without treatment and healing. Affairs are hard for couples to bounce back from because of the trust factor. Trust is the basis for any healthy relationship. Adultery is a cancer that eats away at the fabric of trust.

Arguments

When couples argue constantly it puts a strain on their closeness. The two of them begin to drift farther apart because they can't seem to agree. It is mentioned in the book of Amos how important it is for people to agree before they can walk together. "Can two people walk together without agreeing on the direction?" (Amos 3:3, NLT).

Grudges

It is stated in 1 Corinthians 13 that love keeps no record of wrong, but sometimes spouses do. When a spouse becomes angry, he or she has a tendency to become "historical." During an argument, spouses begin to pull up everything the other did since the day they married. Grudges are evidence that a spouse has not gotten over some trespass because he or she keeps bringing it up. That grudge will forever be a dividing wall in the relationship until the angry spouse learns how to abolish it with forgiveness.

Busyness

Couples are busier than ever because of work schedules, taking care of children, and the everyday tasks of life. Sometimes it is hard to find time for each other after spending so much time trying to make a living for their family.

There was a professor who challenged his class about the importance of time. He had a cylinder and a table with big rocks, small pebbles, sand, and water. He put the big rocks in the cylinder and asked the class if it was full. Some said, "Yes." He then added the smaller pebbles and asked the class if it was full. Fewer said yes because they were second-guessing their reasoning after the first example. After that, he added some sand and asked if it was full. The class, catching on now, said, "No!" He then added the water and it found room as it soaked the sand, traveled through the air between the rocks and pebbles, finally filling the cylinder to capacity.

The professor explained to the class that they would have more time. Nevertheless, they could fill their lives with more meaning if they put the big rocks in first.

Marriage is the big rock. If spouses don't put it in first, the husband and wife both will become a couple of busybodies.

Depression

When a spouse is depressed, he or she can be fully functional and the other spouse will not even know that he or she is wrestling with something so devastating that it separates the two of you emotionally. Some people struggle with seasonal depression while others struggle with clinical depression. Both types can affect how couples communicate. If depression goes undetected, the non-depressed spouse can think that the depressed spouse is just not interested, when in actuality, he or she needs a helping hand to come out of the depression.

In Genesis 30, Jacob couldn't understand when Rachel was depressed because she couldn't give him any children. "When Rachel saw that she was not bearing Jacob any children, she became jealous of her sister. So she said to Jacob, 'Give me children, or I'll die!' Jacob became angry with her and said, 'Am I in the place of God, who has kept you from having children?'" (verses 1-2, NIV).

Women can become depressed because they feel like less than a woman for being unable to do things they think that a woman should do—get pregnant, cook, satisfy her man, etc. Men also can feel depressed when they feel unable to live up to society's standards of what a man should be. For example, when a man has difficulty finding employment and his wife is working, he may sink into depression or become emotionally distant because his manhood feels threatened.

Low Sex Drive

It seems in every relationship there is one spouse who has a higher sex drive than the other. The key to closing this gap is for couples to learn how to satisfy each other's needs. The needs of a man are different from the needs of a woman. Many books have been written on meeting the needs of the both sexes—including *His Needs, Her Needs,* by Willard F. Harley Jr., *The Five Love Languages,* by Gary Chapman, and *Venus and Mars in the Bedroom,* by Dr. John Gray—affirming that different needs exist for the genders.

The truth is that no one is always going to feel like having sex, feel like being affectionate, or feel like talking, but both husbands and wives must learn how to act their way into a feeling. Spouses must learn how to do the things that the other spouse needs, knowing that reciprocity comes from clear communication of needs and taking action to fulfill those needs.

Lack of Spiritual Intimacy

Deuteronomy 22:10 (NIV) reads, "Do not plow with an ox and a donkey yoked together." Often in marriage it seems that couples are pulling at different levels. The ox represents one spouse who is stronger than the donkey spouse. The ox is strong because he or she is in the Word of God and in prayer regularly, while the other spouse lags behind. The donkey spouse is naturally strong, but not as strong as he or she could be if both spouses were on the same spiritual level.

It is so important for spouses to worship together, pray together, and read the Bible together so that they can be on the same page spiritually. Dr. Alvin O'Neal Jackson often has said that when married couples pray it will be hard for them to argue because, if Jesus is in the husband and Jesus is in the wife, it is hard for Jesus to argue with Jesus.

Lack of Romance

Before two people get married, they date. When people date, they put their best foot forward and try to charm their way into the life of the other person. Men open doors. Women put on their most figure-flattering outfit. Both may write love notes or send flowers—all in an effort to romance their mate.

My wife and I went on a vacation to San Juan, Puerto Rico. She had requested that we go somewhere romantic; but more than that, she had asked me to be more consistent in my gestures of thoughtfulness. She said, "Don't just open my door when you are around your family or church members. Do it when we are alone." Every time we go out to eat, I am intentional about sliding my wife's chair out for her. Every time I do, she beams with a smile and says, "I like that, Baby." I didn't know how much of a deposit that was into my wife's love bank account until I started doing it. Those little romance tokens go a long way in ensuring that the emotional distance is bridged in relationship.

Rejection

When I was in college, I got a job as a telemarketer for Olan Mills Portrait Studios. My job was to call people and ask them about purchasing a photography package. I only lasted a day because people kept hanging up on me. I hate rejection. I told the supervisor I would not be coming back the next day.

When your spouse feels that he or she is constantly rejected, it makes it hard for him or her to come back and try again the next day. After repeated rejection, your spouse will become emotionally distant, making room for snakes to come in. Affairs often begin because an outsider can sense when the neglected spouse is starved for attention and he or she is more than willing to give it. This is why it is important for spouses to connect both emotionally and sexually so that they will not give the devil a foothold.

Not Asking for What You Want

It is so important for couples to learn how to ask for what they want from each other. When they don't, their frustration builds to the point that it leads to arguments, grudges, depression, etc. Many times a person knows what he or she wants, but doesn't know how to articulate it. Instead, he or she becomes emotionally clumsy and stumbles over his or her words. What should be a simple request becomes a burning desire that is never revealed because the husband or wife doesn't know how to articulate those needs. If we are going to get back to being naked and unashamed, we must close the emotional gap so that we can please our partners.

When couples are effective in communicating their desires to each other, they are more apt to return to a place where they are naked and without shame. When married couples learn how to communicate and give each other what they need, they will then be able to express what it is that they long for sexually. Sex is more than a ritual that married couples endure grudgingly or out of a sense of marital obligation. Sexual intimacy is designed by God to be a spiritual experience that embodies all three loves—the erotic, the relational and the sacrificial.

When a man and a woman learn how to connect to each other's most precious thoughts and feelings, both spouses can reignite passion and discover euphoria grounded in a spiritual inheritance designed by God to be a part of marriage. Let's go back and discover this bliss.

The husband should not deprive his wife of sexual intimacy, which is her right as a married woman, nor should the wife deprive her husband. The wife gives authority over her body to her husband, and the husband also gives authority over his body to his wife.
(1 Corinthians 7:3-4, NLT)

CHAPTER EIGHT
The Need to Please

"The husband should not deprive his wife of sexual intimacy, which is her right as a married woman, nor should the wife deprive her husband. The wife gives authority over her body to her husband, and the husband also gives authority over his body to his wife. So do not deprive each other of sexual relations. The only exception to this rule would be the agreement of both husband and wife to refrain from sexual intimacy for a limited time, so they can give themselves more completely to prayer. Afterward they should come together again so that Satan won't be able to tempt them because of their lack of self-control" (1 Corinthians 7:3-5, NLT).

It is a Christian couple's responsibility to please each other sexually. This should be a commandment that Christians have the most fun fulfilling. Once misconceptions and issues of shame regarding sex are dealt with, the couple can discover a new world of sexual intimacy. Once the chains are dropped from sexual interpretations, the couple is liberated to explore their sexuality with each other.

Both men and women desire sex, but they approach it differently. Men are very visual and sensual, whereas women hold their sexuality until they can develop a sufficient level of trust to feel safe enough to release it. Often men and women are frustrated because they don't know how to please each other, even though the desire to be pleased lies deep within.

Men need to see their wives naked and unashamed. When Adam first saw Eve, he immediately connected with her, calling Eve, "bone of my bone and flesh of my flesh." Adam saw Eve naked and he was excited. Men need to see their wives and connect with them as "flesh of my flesh." It was out of Adam that Eve was taken, and when he awakened he saw her.

Men must work in reverse to get back inside themselves. It starts with the flesh but it goes much deeper than that. In order for a man to get in touch with himself, he has to touch his woman. In a real sense, when a man enters his wife, he is getting in touch with himself. Therefore, in order for a man to get in touch with his inner emotions, he must be able to enter his wife. Great sex allows the husband to get back to himself and to be close to his wife. That is why it is important that a man connect with his wife sexually so that he can truly be in touch with his inner emotions.

Men, your woman needs to have your ear and your affection before she can open up. The first thing Eve heard was her husband's voice when he gave her affection: "bone of my bone and flesh of my flesh." What messed up their union is when Adam was silent and the serpent came in to deceive Eve. Ever since that time, Eve has been trying to get back her husband's voice and to rid the serpent's deceptive voice from her head.

Affection is the road back to a woman's sexuality. She can't be comfortable in her flesh because of the mess the serpent got her in. When she can hear the man again it puts them side by side again, naked and unashamed.

It is one thing to have a theological understanding of sex and to rid yourselves of shame, but it is another matter entirely to understand how to please one another sexually. For the sake of marital harmony and stability, Christian couples have to know how to please each other.

In his book, *The Power of Five*, Harold Bloomfield, M.D. reveals that regular sexual activity is vital for maintaining higher estrogen levels in women. Higher estrogen has been associated with better bones, better cardiovascular health, and a feeling of joy in life. Men who experience regular sex have a higher testosterone level, which leads to greater confidence, vitality, strength, and energy.

Sex has tremendous power to bring couples closer or push them apart. To fulfill your spouse in bed, new skills are required. Without a clear understanding of the different gender requirements in sex—after a few years, and sometimes only months—sex becomes routine and mechanical. By making a few but significant shifts, couples can overcome this pattern.

Most of the sex education handouts in grade school health classes teach us about our internal reproductive organs. That education is necessary, but so is education regarding our sexual organs and their unique responses to stimulation and desire. As important as it is for our children to become educated about their sexuality, the sad reality is that many adults are not educated about their own bodies. Adam and Eve knew their bodies. They were naked and unashamed. Once Christians have overcome the personal mental and emotional barriers to a flawed sexuality, it is time to put them in touch with their own bodies as well as the body of their spouse.

When people are liberated out of so-called "puritanical mindsets" regarding what it means to be sexual, they are free to explore what it means to please their marital partner. Having been married for over fifteen years, it has been a wonderful journey getting to know my wife. We are now at a place in our lives where we can "touch and agree" on how to please one another. That journey took years of building trust and being able to open up to one another to ask for what we wanted. We both carried our own understanding about sexuality: my own flawed from a promiscuous past during my adolescent years; and hers restricted by a lack of information from her parents. We both were raised with the double standard that it was acceptable for men to "sow their wild oats," while good girls remained chaste until they got married. What happens with these unrealistic expectations more often than not is that you get two unequally yoked individuals struggling with how to please one another.

My wife and I had to wrestle with what is acceptable as a Christian couple and redeem what for the longest had been deemed as "nasty." The most important way to ask for what you want is through the Imago Dialogue, a process through which a couple engages in a structured conversation that enables each partner to extend themselves to understand the experience of the other as different from their own. Interestingly enough, when Adam and Eve were created, the Bible states that God created them in His image. *Imago Dei* is Greek for "the image of God." We were made in the image of God. Adam and Eve were made in the image of God.

Dr. Tammy Nelson has extended the concept of Dr. Harville Hendrix and his wife, Dr. Helen Hunt, who created the Imago Dialogue. Dr. Nelson has established a system of communication wherein couples ask for the sex they desire. Often Christians have thoughts, desires, or fantasies that plague their minds, but they are afraid to pursue them because they consider those actions unclean. When you are not able to address these thoughts or desires to your spouse there is a danger that he or she may turn to outlets that can lead to sexual perversions like pornography, adultery, incest, homosexuality, swinging, etc. When you are able to express the desires of your heart to your spouse, through the Imago Dialogue technique, he or she is able to listen to you without judgment.

Here is an example of how to use Dr. Nelson's *Imago Dialogue* (Nelson, 2008):

Step One

First, choose who will be the "sender" and who will be the "receiver." The senders will tell their partner the following:

• What you always wanted to try sexually.

The receiver will simply repeat (or mirror) what the sender says. It is important in an empathic dialogue that you don't add any of your own reactivity, and mirror exactly what your partner sends over. The following conversation is an example of what it is like for couples to discuss a sensitive issue through Imago Dialogue.

Sender: "I have always wanted us to try having sex in the shower."

The receiver simply mirrors back, maintaining eye contact, "So, you have always wanted us to try having sex together in the shower."

There are only two possible responses receivers need to make at this point. Either "Please send that again," or "Is there more?" At that point, the sender can respond "Yes" and send more information, or "No" and stop there.

Step Two

Sender: "I would really like to give you a slow, sensual back rub."

Receivers mirror back what the senders said.

Step Three

Sender: "My sexual fantasy is for me to touch myself while you watch."

Receivers mirror back what the senders said.

Step Four

After the sender has communicated all their desires and the receiver has mirrored them back, the receiver summarizes all of them by saying, "So what I heard you say was..."

Step Five

The receiver then validates each statement, starting with, "It makes sense to me you would want to try...knowing you the way I know you, I can understand why you would desire that." This format makes validation easier.

Step Six

Now it is time for the receiver to empathize, which means to guess at what you think your partner would feel if he or she had these desires and fantasies fulfilled. For example:

Receiver: "I can imagine that if we did those things it would make you feel… (add feelings). Is there anything more you want?"

Step Seven

At this stage, the couple switches, giving your partner an opportunity to summarize, validate, and empathize.

If that moment is not a good time, or if further dialogue is needed to find empathy, request an alternate time to talk further about your desires and fantasies. Make a plan to keep talking until you both feel openness and trust in the relationship. There is no need to rush; just hearing about each other's sexual and erotic desires might add enough spark and excitement that making love spontaneously is a definite possibility!

This dialogue process can help you both discover the passion and the erotic energy needed for great sex. You will, through this exercise, come to understand normal erotic curiosity. The term "erotic curiosity" is simply a way to define human thoughts, fantasies, and sexual desires. It is perfectly normal for human beings to have curiosity about things that are sexual, and most people explore erotic thoughts and fantasies in their minds all the time, even if they don't share these thoughts with their partner. Understanding your partner's erotic fantasy life will help you understand what will make him or her happy and gives you clues about what will give you both a passionate, loving partnership.

Understanding Sexual Empathy

Establishing sexual empathy does not mean your partner will agree with your thoughts and fantasies or want to act them out with you. Sexual empathy instead means that you understand that these are your partner's erotic thoughts, and not your own. Empathy also includes being happy that your partner feels safe enough to share them with you. Feeling safe to share your fantasies is a big step toward finding passion and establishing a connection in your relationship. It is a step toward being naked and unashamed.

People can only share their fantasies when they feel safe and respected. If you know that your partner will listen and mirror back your thoughts and feelings without judgment, then you will be more likely to share your most intimate thoughts and desires. Sexual empathy means your partner will listen to your erotic thoughts and hold that space as a sacred trust.

Undoubtedly, some will ask, "Isn't it dangerous to share your sexual fantasies with your spouse?" The reality is that you are thinking about it anyway, and yes, you can repress those fantasies, hoping they will go away. Actually, repressing those feelings tends to make them more dominant in your mind, rather than causing them to go away.

Sharing your most intimate thoughts and feelings with your spouse puts your fantasies on the table. It would have been great if Eve had been able to come back home and tell Adam, "I'm thinking of biting from the forbidden tree." Our lives might be different today if Eve had shared her feelings before committing the deed!

When you share your temptations and desires with your spouse, several different things are likely to happen. One spouse will have a desire and follows through without involving or informing the other. Or, one spouse can lead the other one into an act that can be detrimental to the relationship. But there is, I believe, a third option. A husband and wife should be able to dialogue about what the other desires to do, even when it is not acceptable. Eve should have been able to say what she was thinking about. Adam should have voiced disagreement when Eve invited him to bite into the forbidden fruit.

When two people who are in Christ and are prayed up, Scripture reveals that Jesus will be in the midst of them. Christians fear that even talking about their fantasies will give the green light to pursue the forbidden and lead to exile from the garden of right relationship. This does not have to be the case.

In *Every Woman's Battle* (WaterBrook Press, 2003), author Shannon Ethridge brings up a good point as it relates to sexual integrity. Fantasies left alone in the mind of women can lead to deceptive strongholds. Fantasies can lead to sexual compromise that may cause married couples to drift beyond the boundaries of what is acceptable to God.

Ethridge writes, "When you fantasize about someone else when making love with your husband, you are mentally making love with another man. He, not your husband, is the one you feel passionate about. He, not your husband, is the one you feel close to emotionally."[1]

Sometimes the purpose of sharing sexual fantasies with your spouse can be to let him or her know your thoughts about the forbidden. But at other times sharing can inform him or her about a tree that is not forbidden, it is just that you have not yet had a chance to eat from this particular tree. Ethridge's point is to make sure that every woman and man monitors who and what enters into the garden of their minds.

Using the Imago Dialogue as a communication tool, couples can open up discussion and come to an agreement about what is acceptable and not acceptable. That which you both agree is acceptable before God, use it in your bedroom. That which is an abomination, don't use it but try to have empathy for your spouse and give credence to how he or she arrived at that desire. For example, suppose a wife tells her husband that she has fantasies about being with another man. The couple can use the Imago Dialogue technique to help the husband empathize with her fantasy. Then, at a later time, when both are ready to discuss the fantasy further, he can ask open-ended questions about how she arrived to the point of wanting to be with another man. Their dialogue could lead to the revelation that he has not been giving her the attention she desires and that the other man has been showering her with compliments at work. These dialogues are excellent opportunities for couples to improve upon their skills to please each other.

I had a pastor tell me jokingly that he loved his wife so much that if he caught her with another man, he would tell them, "Hold it right there!"

Then he explained how he would get a camera and take a picture, because, he said, "Obviously, there's something he's doing that I'm not!" Now, this is not something I would encourage. Nevertheless, the point of his joke is that the mental pictures wives and husbands have in their minds are images that couples can learn from—not to endorse with blind acceptance, but rather, to study as clues to improving their marital relationship.

Every couple can improve their marital relationship in general, and their sex life in particular. It takes intentional effort and open communication. Pray for your spouse that he or she is able to shift those energies back to a healthier and holier use of the erotic. If need be, encourage them to get help for those areas that may not align with what you both agree is not healthy or holy.

Growth comes from what you bring to a relationship, not what you get out of it. When you create an atmosphere of non-judgmental trust and give your spouse what he or she really wants, you both grow into fully realized individuals.

Do you not know that your bodies are members of Christ himself? Shall I then take the members of Christ and unite them with a prostitute? Never! Do you not know that he who unites himself with a prostitute is one with her in body? For it is said,
"the two will become one flesh."
(1 Corinthians 6:15-16, NIV)

CHAPTER NINE
What He Wants...What She Wants

Sexual intercourse is not the only way for a husband and wife to connect on a deep level; it is also a sure way to help establish a lasting bond in the marriage. When a man and a woman connect sexually, they also connect spiritually.

The act of sexual intercourse is more than just physical; it is spiritual and emotional. The apostle Paul cautioned in 1 Corinthians 6:15-16: "Do you not know that your bodies are members of Christ himself? Shall I then take the members of Christ and unite them with a prostitute? Never! Do you not know that he who unites himself with a prostitute is one with her in body? For it is said, 'The two will become one flesh'" (NIV).

Researchers have concluded that a woman releases a chemical known as oxytocin when she has sex with a man that makes her emotionally bond with him. No matter how much people say that human beings can separate emotions from sexuality, it is simply not true. When Jesus healed the woman with the issue of blood and she touched Him, Jesus right away recognized that someone had "touched" Him—not in a sexual way, but rather in a physical way that drained Him spiritually.

When men and women connect sexually they connect in other ways that are far deeper. The Bible uses the word "know" to describe the union between a man and a woman when they have intercourse. Isn't it interesting that they used the word know? It is stated in Genesis 4:1 (KJV), "Adam knew Eve his wife; and she conceived, and bare Cain, and said, I have gotten a man from the LORD."

The Hebrew word for "know" means "to know, care about, choose; to make known, involving intelligent worship, obedience, etc.; of God's knowing persons, etc., thoroughly; knowing the heart; knowing his true servants, recognizing and acknowledging them; take notice of, regard; know of Israel as chosen people; know of a person *obj.* (of sodomy).

The concise Hebrew and Aramaic lexicon offers several definitions for know as it appears in the Old Testament: 1. observe, realize (Genesis 3:7; Exodus 2:4); find out how it is with (Esther 2:11); 2. find out [through information, communication] (2 Samuel 24:2); experience (Isaiah 47:8); 3. recognize, perceive [from observation, deliberation] (Genesis 15:8); know [perceive] that I am YHWH [God] (Exodus 6:7); 4. care about, be concerned about (Genesis 39:6;).

All of these results come from sexual connection—observing one's sexual partner, finding out who that person really is. Through the sexual experience both begin to embrace deeper levels of the person's psyche and perceive another side of them. That is why the old saying is true: "To know me is to love me."

If their intercourse is not mutually pleasing, however, it will be more difficult for a deeper, spiritual connection to take place.

Part of good lovemaking includes understanding what the other desires. Truly knowing each other's likes and desires is a process. Great sex without such knowing can happen every now and then, but consistently good sex requires more than chance. It is determined by knowing what turns the other spouse on—a process that begins before entering the bedroom.

Both men and women are guilty of assuming what the other wants. Such assumptions can make for disastrous sex. To make sure you and your spouse stay connected, you must keep romance in your relationship and understand what turns your mate on.

One of the first things husbands and wives need to know about sexual anatomy is that there are significant differences in how men and women become sexually stimulated. Couples miss out on the full degree of joy they could be experiencing when they make assumptions about what arouses and stimulates each other.

The Art of Kissing

Kissing is a lost art. We all can remember our first kiss and the excitement that it brought. Kissing was really a celebration when you graduated to the "French kiss." There is something very passionate about a good kiss. Often in marriage, couples settle into obligatory pecks with no passion. When two people are strongly attracted to the each other that first kiss is electric. It feels like trying to pull the lips off of and suck the tongue right out of the other person's mouth.

Because men are often the aggressors and initiators in the relationship, they like it when a woman initiates the kiss. When a woman grabs a man's face around his ears and pulls his face to hers, it makes him feel as if he is the most desired and attractive man in the universe. The thought that goes through the chambers of his mind is, "This woman really wants me!"

By contrast, women love delicate kisses throughout the day. She likes it when her man walks up behind her at the kitchen sink and lightly kisses her neck. Or when he spins her around, kisses her in the mouth, and tells her "I love you," and then walks away. Women love romance and men love to be ravished. Kisses do work!

Good Hygiene Practices

Cleanliness is very essential to attraction and good sex for both men and women. Men have a tendency to want to run into the bedroom without showering from a busy day. One of the biggest turn-offs for a woman is to perform oral sex, or to be down by the penis and smell the leftover scent of a busy day! Before your bedroom time, each of you should shower and thoroughly clean all areas of the genitalia—scrotum, buttocks, vagina, etc. It also helps to shave the pubic area. Hair in the pubic area is a matter preference, but the smoother the pubic area the less you are slowed down by hair follicles getting in your mouth. A couple can make cleansing and shaving more fun and arousing by taking a shower or bath together.

The cleaner and sweeter you smell before lovemaking, the more your spouse will want to gobble you up! After you bathe properly, apply some sensual smelling lotions and perfumes to your body. A light scent is usually best—nothing overpowering.

Men should clip their toenails and get a manicure. When a man places his fingers in or around the vagina, a hangnail can disturb the rhythm of the moment and take the woman out of her arousal. It doesn't hurt to get a pedicure, either. No woman is turned on by scratchy, rusty feet!

When a woman comes to bed, she needs to let her man ogle her. He wants to see her in the fullness of her beauty and appreciate her. Sometimes a woman has to take certain measures to make sure that her man can appreciate her beauty and not be turned off by curlers, bonnets, and scarves. African-American women in particular have a need to sleep with a head scarf to protect their investment of going to the beauty salon. Every man appreciates his woman's attempt to have beautiful hair, but rollers and scarves are not sexy. A good compromise is that the woman can come to bed with her hair down. When the lovemaking is over and the husband is nodding off, she can slip back into the bathroom and tie her head up in the silk scarf that is needed to preserve her perm. Or, she can try sleeping on a satin pillowcase if she is too tired to get up.

What Turns Him On

In order to please the man, a woman needs to know one thing. Men derive much of their pleasure from their penis. Women work against themselves when they caress and rub men all over their bodies but avoid the penis. Women would save themselves a great deal of frustration if they would learn how to go straight toward the pleasure center of men—the penis.

A perceptive woman will notice that first thing in the morning, one of her husband's hands mysteriously disappears under the covers. He will be asleep with his hands in his pants. It is just part of being a male. If a boy child is observed before waking up in the morning, he likely will be caught in the same sleeping position. From a very early age, a male becomes very much acquainted with his penis. In fact, male babies experience their first erection within hours after they are born.

Many jokes are made about a man's obsession with his penis, but a man's attachment to his sexual organ is rarely off track or exaggerated.

Visual Stimuli

It is no real secret that men are visual. When a man is stimulated visually, then he is aroused by what he sees. He will be stimulated by what his wife looks like. Watching her turns him on. That is why it is important for women to dress up and wear sexy lingerie in the bedroom. Many women think, "Why bother to wear sexy lingerie? He's not going to let me keep it on very long!" A woman needs to know one thing: It's not about how long she keeps it on. It's all about variety!

Men like the feeling of conquering something. Taking off his woman's clothes gives a man a sense of having conquered—taking off the clothes of something new. It is the same woman, but the variety revives the spark in the relationship and helps couples avoid the routine of sex.

Auditory Stimuli

Some men are enticed by sound. The sounds of lovemaking will excite men, who are auditory. Listening to the soft sounds of his wife's pleasure or hearing her scream with passion will send him over the edge! Sensual music, poetry read aloud, and the sound of "dirty talk" spoken in his wife's voice will turn him on.

As a man realizes that his wife's excitement is growing, he will naturally want to give her more of the same. A man needs to be careful of "going harder" when his wife responds verbally to his stimulation of her. For example, as it relates to oral sex, just because a wife moans with pleasure doesn't mean that she wants her husband to "go harder" with the same technique. Going harder doesn't necessarily lead a woman to orgasm. It can actually have the reverse effect. Going harder may cause a woman to lose her arousal because of the sensitive nature of the clitoris. Since most of the nerve endings around the vagina are on the inner lips (*labia minora*), a man can be more effective by applying the right touch and light stroking rather than by simply pounding into a woman.

Male Anatomy 101: Male Genitalia

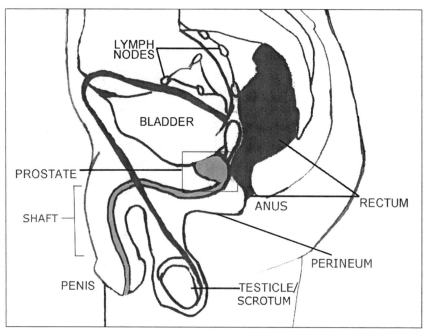

Part of a woman knowing how to please her husband lies in her knowing his body and how it works. There are different parts of the penis that women should familiarize themselves with.

Scrotum

It is the protective sack where his testicles reside. This is a very sensitive spot for a man, so a woman needs to be careful when touching this area. It really pleasures a man for his wife to touch him with a feathery touch, but too much pressure can be unpleasant.

Shaft

This is the "rod" that connects the head to the scrotum. When a man is aroused, the penis shaft swells with blood, adding several inches to its length.

Head

The helmet-shaped tip of the penis is where a lot of the nerve endings are. When a woman is performing oral sex on her husband, it is important that she never let her teeth touch this part. In fact, biting of any kind is a turn-off for most men.

Urethra

This is primarily a functional hole for urine to be expelled. It is generally quite irritating for men to have any kind of stimulus directly inside of the urethra.

Frenulum

This part of the penis can be detected around the ridge of the penis. It makes a V shape on the underside of his penis. When the woman focuses attention on this area it can speed up the ejaculation of the man because it is so sensitive.

Ridge

The ring at the base of the head is the most sensitive part of the penis. Many women concentrate on taking in the entire penis in their mouths when the attention needs to be around the head and the ridge.

Testicles

Webster's Dictionary defines them as "typically paired male reproductive glands that produce sperm and secrete testosterone." While some men like having their testicles lightly sucked, biting, squeezing, and hitting are not recommended. The testicles are very sensitive.

Anus

The anus has a high concentration of nerve endings that can be engaged to bring a man pleasure. When a woman stimulates the anus in conjunction with oral or hand play it can enhance the pleasure of her man.

Perineum

It is the area between the testicles and the anus. It is close enough to the prostate so that when pressure is applied, it can intensify a man's orgasm.

Chest and Nipples

After the woman has been successful in pleasing the penis, then the blood flowing to the rest of the man's body makes him even more receptive to touch. There are endorphins that numb the pain sensors in the body so that nipples can be nibbled, sucked, and even pinched if the man so desires. Sometimes men don't know they like something until the woman initiates it. But it is important to attempt new techniques only after he has been satisfied through penile stimulation.

Prostate

The prostate gland or "P-spot" is above the perineum and inside the anal wall. This area has as many nerve endings, as does the woman's G-spot, and is many times equivalent in sensitivity. The prostate, when stimulated, enhances pleasure for men and can cause orgasm and ejaculation.

There are two ways to stimulate the prostate. One is to insert a well-lubricated finger into the anus and reach up about two inches, feeling for a round ball approximately the size of a golf ball. The prostate can be smaller or larger, depending on health and heredity. Before inserting a finger into the anus, the woman should be sure to have lots of water-based lubricant on the finger and around the anus area. Go slowly, and only with permission.

The second way to stimulate the prostate is through prostate massage. Because the prostate is on the perineum—the area between the scrotum and the anus—outer massage can be done without going through the anus.

Some men are hesitant about allowing themselves to feel the powerful sensations of prostate pleasure if they equate anal pleasure with homosexuality. However, most men, if this is done correctly, will enjoy the sensations.

Fellatio (Oral Sex)

A man can be aroused by the sight and sounds of his wife performing fellatio. In his mind she is enjoying giving him pleasure. Every man wants to believe that his wife is hungry for his penis, as it states in Song of Songs 2:3 (NIV):

> Beloved
> "Like an apple tree among the trees of the forest
> is my lover among the young men.
> I delight to sit in his shade,
> and his fruit is sweet to my taste."

When a woman is performing oral sex on her husband, she should imagine she is eating her favorite Popsicle® in the heat of the day. If it is not eaten fast enough, it will melt. The temptation is to slurp all of the melting juices before they slide down the shaft of the Popsicle® and drop to the floor. Then the woman licks all the way down and slurps, careful not to waste a drop. That is how a wife should approach her man's penis, and all the while moaning with sure delight as she enjoys the fruit of her husband that is sweet to her taste.

To add variety, couples can enhance the taste by using gels of different flavors, fruit, whip cream, peanut butter, chocolate sauce, etc. Breath strips can also be fun. They not only help with the taste, they also add a cooling sensation to the skin of the husband's penis. The man can also use these strips after they have fully aroused the clitoris. Using these strips adds a cooling sensation by blowing on the skin that has been sucked.

Oral sex is one of the ways a woman can directly give her love to a man. Oral sex can be a beautiful gift of her love for him, or it can leave her with an uncomfortable feeling. Here are some ways that husbands can help to eliminate that discomfort:

1. The husband should not grab his wife's head and ram when he is close to orgasm. Men have a tendency to become aggressive when they are aroused. When a man feels pleasure during oral sex and wants to avoid the urge to grab his wife's head, he should simply put his hands down by his side or behind his own head.

2. A man should not expect his wife to swallow; that is at her discretion.

3. Learning how to rest her jaw and use her hands can help ease a woman's discomfort. When a husband is enjoying oral sex, chances are his eyes will be closed and he will not notice her using her hand. A well-lubricated hand feels just as good as a warm mouth. A wife can alternate without her husband knowing (or caring) which one she is using.

4. Once she has stimulated his penis for a while, the rest of his body becomes much more sensuous. To increase his pleasure, she can then begin to spread the pleasure out around his body.

Marcy Michaels and Marie Desalle have written two good books to help couples learn how to perform oral sex: *The Lowdown on Going Down: How to Give Her Mind-Blowing Oral Sex*, and *Blow Him Away:*

How to Give Him Mind-Blowing Oral Sex. Furthermore, the Internet has a plethora of resources on oral sex techniques.

Some African Americans are still reticent to engage in oral sex, even among married couples. That said, sometimes there is too much stock placed on oral sex. The hand of a woman stroking a man's penis can be just as effective, if not more so, than the mouth. In their book, The *Handjob Handbook*, Marsha Normandy and Joseph St. James give a detailed explanation on how to incorporate over twenty-five different hand jobs. The authors state that: "You must disabuse yourself of the notion that the Hand Job is somehow a lowly consolation prize compared to the lofty hummer. A hand job offers your man an entirely different sensory experience than oral sex. It's a separate skill set—and if you get good at it, he might just ask you to give your mouth a rest."[1]

What Turns Her On

I own a classic car—a 1966 Chevy Impala. It is a two-door classic, silver, with black tweed interior. I've put a lot of money into that car. It has a 350 corvette engine, 24-inch tires, stereo, GPS, power steering, A/C.

As much as I love my car, however, I cannot handle it like I do more modern cars. In fact, when I rented a new Volvo, I almost couldn't drive it off the Hertz parking lot because I couldn't figure out the push-button features! To start the Volvo, all I had to do was press the brake and push a button and the motor immediately started humming. Not so with the 1966 Impala. Depending on the weather, I might have to spend a little more time getting it started. If it is warm, my classic beauty may start easier, but then I may need to adjust the carburetor because too much gas might flood it. In winter, I have to pump the gas pedal a little bit so the cold gas lines can get some fuel to the carburetor. Then, after she gets to chugging steadily, I have to let her sit in the garage and warm up to a hum in the cold winter air. She's beautiful, but temperamental. But once she gets going, it is like driving a jet engine down the interstate and every man wishes he had her.

Being married to a woman is a lot like the privilege of owning a classic car. She is so beautiful and capable of revving up to great speeds, but a man has to know how to handle her. A man has to know that he can't just get in and push a button and think that he is going to take off with her. He first has to gauge the weather. The temperature determines how he will approach the startup. Many men want to approach having sex with their wives like the new push-button Volvo. Women have evolved over the centuries, but one thing has stayed the same: it takes time to get her aroused.

Think More like a Woman

There's a very old saying: "Why can't a woman be more like a man?" When it comes to sexual intercourse, men are often guilty of treating women as though they will respond like a man. I had the privilege of sitting down for dinner with my wife and another couple engaged in full-time ministry. I told them I was working on a book to help Christian married couples improve their sexual relationship. The question I needed help with was, "What are the things that turn a woman on, and what are the things that turn a woman off?" The two women looked at me with intrigue and apprehension. My wife said, "Each woman is different, but there are some things that are universal." We began our discussion.

Turn Offs

The women proceeded to talk about what turns a woman off. Many men mistakenly think that the things that turn them on will turn on women as well. Men are stimulated by direct and immediate contact with the genitalia. Many men are also fixated with the breasts. These are two places on a woman's body that men immediately make contact with—because they are thinking like men.

In reality, women like to be approached gently and romantically. Like the classic car, they have to be warmed up before they can go speeding down the highway. Women need foreplay. They need to be touched gently. I was reading an article in *Men's Health* magazine that offered an example of touching and starting off slowly:

Prop yourself up with pillows and have her sit so that she's facing away from you and leaning back against your chest. Reach around and use your fingertips or the flat of your hand along and between her legs in up-and-down, side-to-side, and figure-8 moves. The Gain: This position is easy to maintain, enhances intimacy, and helps her relax—that way you can both be more effective. Your other hand will be free to run over the rest of her body.[2]

Women are turned on by touch, or kinesthetic arousal. The feel of things on her body is arousing. Since women are kinesthetic, touch engages them sexually more than other senses do. Touching her, feeling her skin, and holding her will be important to her for experiencing pleasure.

Any stimulation that creates a kinesthetic response—massages, feathers, feather dusters, ice cubes—will make a woman feel passionate and alive.

Another "don't" for men to remember is that touching doesn't always lead to sex. If a wife thinks that the only time her husband touches her is when he wants sex, his caresses will have an adverse affect. She will be repulsed by his touch rather than excited. Sometimes a man needs to just massage his wife's feet without wanting anything but showing her affection.

When a husband is affectionate, his wife is turned on because it shows that he cares for her. Women don't like to be treated like walking vaginas. A wife wants to know that her husband cares about how she feels and what she thinks. Overall, she wants to know that she has influence in her husband's life, and he shows her that she does when he is affectionate.

Finally, women hate it when men start out pounding and going fast with sexual activity. Whether it is oral sex or intercourse, women want to start slow and gentle. Men must learn the discipline of starting gently with a feathery touch before increasing the intensity of their pace or their touch. Men sometimes mistake the groans of satisfaction as a cue to increase the intensity. Especially as it relates to the clitoris, the man must learn that it is a sensitive part of the vagina. When he overstimulates the clitoris the woman loses feeling or becomes agitated, which takes away her ability to reach orgasm.

Thought or Cognitive

The stimulation of the female imagination can also be arousing. In other words, sexual fantasies can get her hot. When spouses think about each other and imagine different positions, it will stimulate the cognitive mind.

Women romanticize in their minds. There are thoughts that take place in a woman's mind that she may never verbalize to her husband. This is why romance novels are so popular with women. Such reading enables them to carry out their fantasies through the fictional characters they put themselves into.

What better way for a husband to engage his wife sexually than to give her something to think about? He can write her letters about what he would like to do with her and to her. He can send her text messages throughout the day that are steamy and detailed. He can call her and have phone sex with her during the day or when one of them is out of town.

The Imago Dialogue is key in this process as well because it is a safe way for a woman to share what is on her mind. The danger here is that a husband may try to move too fast on what his wife shares with him. It will feel like a betrayal of trust if he presses her on acting out on her fantasies before she is ready. Husbands also need to consider whether or not the fantasy or desire is even something they can, in good conscience, bring into the marriage bed.

Dr. Nelson offers a good tool for Christians to use in the Imago Dialogue, but we must be careful that we do not attempt to carry out every fantasy. I like this tool because it creates a safe place for couples to talk about what they are thinking about. If a husband or wife cannot share with his or her spouse, with whom can that person share?

The Imago Dialogue is a tool that opens up the mind and heart for both spouses to explore together what is good and what is to be avoided. God told Adam and Eve they could have anything they wanted in their secret garden except one tree. Couples have to agree upon what tree they are not going to eat from based upon their understanding of Scripture.

There are many components to good lovemaking—communication, affection, respect, and actual physical skill. Part of being skilled at lovemaking includes knowing and understanding each other's anatomy. By divine design, men and women are different and our bodies respond to different stimuli. Improved sexual relations between husbands and wives will depend on each spouse taking the initiative to understand the other's body.

Female Anatomy 101: Female Genitalia

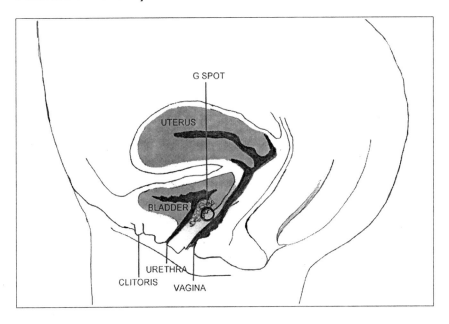

The Vulva

The vulva (the external female genitals) consists of two sets of labia, or lips. These lips are folds of skin that vary in size and elasticity. They are as unique to the individual as any other part of a woman's body.

A man should always have clean hands when he touches his wife's vulva. As he touches her, he should go slowly at first, and be gentle. Touching the sensitive parts of the vulva using dry fingers can catch and drag the skin and cause discomfort, so it is important to use a water-based lubricant.

When choosing a lubricant, it is important to remember that those containing scents or heating effects can cause urinary tract or yeast infections in a woman. Furthermore, any chemical that comes into contact with this area can cause burning, discomfort, and infection.

Labia

The labia swell when a woman is aroused. Sometimes the inner labia hang outside the outer labia and sometimes they are covered. Both are normal, however. Inside the inner labia lies the clitoris at the top. The clitoris is a small projection, approximately the size of a pea, situated above the vagina, at the top of the vulva. The clitoris can project out from between the labia or be hidden in the folds of the labia. Like the size of men's penises, the size of a woman's clitoris will vary.

Urethra

Farther down the vulva is the opening to the vagina, which is the wider part of the female genitalia. Between the clitoris and the vagina is the urethra. The urethra is the opening where women urinate. Women do not urinate from their vagina, even during orgasm.

Also, the urethra is sensitive to bacteria, and nothing should be dragged or rubbed over this area that might carry bacteria from fingers or hands.

The Clitoris

The woman's pleasure center is partially covered by a small flap of skin, or hood. When a woman becomes aroused, the clitoris becomes erect or engorged. Like a penis, the more erect it becomes, the more it wants to be touched.

When a woman is very aroused, her man can stimulate her even more intensely by pressing a couple of fingers just north of the clitoris and then pulling back, fully exposing it. This, however, should be done cautiously. If the clitoris is touched with too much pressure or too soon, she may not be able to have an orgasm, even if she is in the mood. Too much pressure on the clitoris can temporarily numb her sensations. A man should aim to have a feather touch on his wife's genitals.

Dr. John Gray, in *Venus and Mars in the Bedroom*, wrote, "It is very important for a man to remember to go north before he goes south." A man should gently circle the clitoris, always making sure it is lubricated so the friction doesn't cause her pain. While touching the clitoris, he may want to try tracing his fingers over her clitoris as if he is writing out the alphabet. He should carefully note whether certain letters get a bigger response. If his fingers get a little tired, he can simply relax his hands and use his tongue. She will love it! This technique will provide an entirely different sensation.

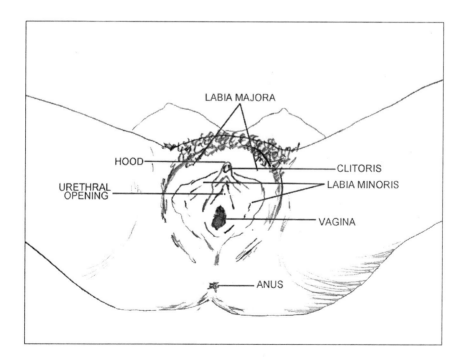

Cunnilingus (Oral Sex)

Some men are still reticent to perform oral sex on a woman, even on their own wife. But skeptical men may feel more comfortable performing oral sex on a woman when he realizes that as long as she keeps herself clean and is healthy, licking her vaginal secretions is quite sanitary. In fact, in the Far East, vaginal secretions were once considered the elixir of immorality.

The goal in performing oral sex is not for the husband to go straight for the vagina as if it is the "touch-down" area. A woman must be warmed up before he can have oral sex with her. When a man approaches his wife's vagina, he must know that it is a very sensitive fruit that must be "peeled" layer by layer. In fact, the man should approach it as if he is searching for an exotic fruit sweet to the taste.

He should start by preparing the area—rubbing her stomach with his fingertips and then caressing her inner thighs. He can then proceed to the vaginal area with his hand going around the outer lips until the outer lips beg to be opened. It will take time for a husband to learn the specific movements that will arouse his wife. As he is discovering her likes and dislikes, he can feel the rhythm of his wife's body and use it as a gauge. If the woman remains rigid and lies still, it could be that she is not enjoying the experience.

Sometimes the issue with cunnilingus lies with the woman and not the man. Some women have been trained that oral sex is nasty, so they push the man away. If a wife is struggling with accepting oral sex as an acceptable form of lovemaking, the husband should use the Imago Dialogue tool to discuss his desire to perform oral sex before attempting to do so. Only if and when both have agreed that this is acceptable should the husband proceed with a gentle touch.

When the woman is fully aroused, her husband can use his tongue or fingers and trace around the outer lips. You can tug with your lips (not your teeth) on the outer lips, kissing them gently. If you use your teeth, you will kill her mood and have to start all over again. Remember: be gentle. After she is beginning to open up and grinding a bit more, suggesting you are in the right spot, then you can take your tongue or fingers around the inner lips. The flat of the tongue is better to start off with instead of going for the more pointed end of your tongue because you need to be sensitive. It is not until the woman is fully aroused that you can apply more pressure.

When your wife is at full arousal her legs will be fully spread and limber. If she is turned off, it will be like pulling a "wishbone" apart on Thanksgiving. When she is fully aroused, you can slowly and gently approach the clitoris with the flat of your tongue. The exposed clitoris is the precious fruit that you have patiently been looking for. It is a precious pearl that must be respected. An easy way to approach it is to trace lightly the letters of the alphabet. Remember: the lighter the better. For some reason men think that harder is better. It is the opposite in the world of women. You should develop a signal between each other to let the other know when to go harder and when to go softer. Maybe softer would be one tap on the leg and harder would be two taps. When the woman is fully aroused, then you can begin to write full sentences with the tip of your tongue. At this phase, you can also use your hands to rub her stomach, her breasts, and even the outer area of her vagina.

The more a woman gets aroused, the more endorphins are released into her body that block pain and she can take more groping than usual. At this point, you may want to lightly pull or squeeze her nipples depending on your wife's personal preference. As you are stimulating the clitoris you can use your free hand and tease the vaginal opening with your thumb. The sensation of stimulating the clitoris and the vaginal opening at the same time will give her dual pleasure. The more she is aroused the more she wants to be touched.

Vagina

The vaginal opening has numerous nerve endings, which makes the opening a place of extreme satisfaction. It has been said that the size of the man's penis is not what matters most, but rather, what he does with it.

In other words, as the old saying goes, "It's not the size of the ship, but the motion of the ocean."

I used to think those were just the words of some woman trying to make her husband feel better about having a small penis. In actuality, there is truth in that statement. If a man learns how to use the ridge of his penis to stimulate the opening of the vaginal canal effectively, he can help her reach climax with that gentle stroke.

The idea is to allow the woman to have her orgasm first. However, the woman may not have an orgasm every time a couple has sex. Because men are goal-oriented, they can become fixated on pleasing the woman to the point that orgasm takes the place of emotionally connecting with her. When a husband has pleased his wife through oral sex and she has reached orgasm, he can still give her stimulation. Women are multiorgasmic, so there is no need to rush past the first orgasm. A husband has to be careful to soften his touch once again to avoid overstimulation of the clitoris or vagina.

Men should learn how to take their time and really experience the emotional connection with the woman during this phase. It is important that a man be intentional on feeling himself inside of his wife. He can begin to connect with her by looking in her eyes and cherishing the gift that God has given him. He can: feel his heartbeat next to hers; allow each other's breathing to coincide; and allow himself to meditate on the words that Adam said: "Finally, bone of my bone and flesh of my flesh."

Anal Sex

Anal sex has always been looked down upon in the church because of the biblical story of Sodom and Gomorrah. The sin in that story was that men wanted to rape the guests of Lot by having anal sex. True enough, anal sex is not a natural function. The anal cavity was meant to expel and not receive. However, there are nerve endings around the anal area that are sensitive to stimuli when aroused.

The preference for anal stimulation and penetration varies from woman to woman. There must be clear communication and trust between a husband and wife before this can take place. It is not something that can be forced upon a woman, as there are serious health risks that can accompany anal sex—both physical and emotional. There can be a ripping of the rectum because of lack of lubrication. A vaginal infection can develop if a bacterium from the anal area gets in the vagina. Furthermore, some women feel that anal sex is degrading. This is another area wherein the Imago Dialogue tool would be helpful to couples in determining acceptable sexual activity.

There is nothing in Scripture that states that a husband and wife cannot have anal sex, but there are natural consequences that would make one think twice before engaging in this form of sexual activity.

When She's Ready

When a woman's engine is fully warmed, she is ready to run. When a woman is fully excited, then she may want the man to increase his thrust or speed up the intensity. The key word is "may." A husband has to be in tune with his wife's disposition. Just like a man can listen to his car's engine and tell if it is idling too high, he has to listen to the body language of his wife. It may help for couples to establish some type of code word or hand gesture that the wife can use to let the man know "harder" or "softer." For example, one tap of the finger on the shoulder might mean softer, two taps might mean harder. Great sex depends on a husband knowing his wife.

A good rule of thumb is to keep it slow and steady until she begs you to increase velocity. Then it is time to take that car down the interstate! Take it slow. When I first put my new engine in my car, I was advised not to go past 55 mph for a certain number of miles. I needed to go slow so the engine could get broken in. Men have the tendency of jumping in the cars and wanting to go 0 to 60 in a matter of seconds. It is against a man's nature to get in a fast car and take his time.

A husband has to remember that his wife is a classic. He has to start slowly. Women want to be treasured. She wants to savor the kiss. She wants her man to look in her eyes at dinner. She wants her husband to touch every part of her body, not just his favorite parts.

Every husband needs to take the time to learn the favorite parts on his wife's body that she likes for him to touch. Surprisingly, or perhaps not, some men don't even know. A fun way to learn is for a husband to spend a night taking inventory of her erogenous zones. The woman has so many places of pleasure to touch, but each woman is different.

Her Head

Stress often originates in the top of the scalp. One of the ways a husband can help his wife relax is massage her scalp with his fingers. I have also seen an apparatus that looks like a long metal granddaddy spider that fits over the scalp for an incredible massage. Some women love to be touched on their scalp and to have their hair slightly stroked. In the intensity of sex, when the endorphins have kicked in some women like to have their hair pulled. Before trying this, a man should check with his wife. Otherwise, he can bring a screeching halt to a wonderful experience by pulling too hard too soon.

Her Face, Neck, and Ears

Some women love their faces touched softly with a glancing touch as her man kisses her. Soft kisses on the side of the neck and sometimes from the back as you kiss her softly on the back of her neck gives the woman a jolt of excitement. She feels vulnerable and romanced at the same time. Some women enjoy it when the man nibbles on her ears, while others may like the tongue in the ear.

Her Shoulders and Collarbone

These are two more places on a woman where a man can nibble and kiss. When a woman is stressed, her shoulders are a good place to massage to relieve stress knots.

Her Back

One of the biggest inhibitors to a blissful night of sex is a stressed-out woman. The back is one of the largest muscles on the body and also a place of stress. When a husband can relax his wife and help to relieve her stress, he enables her to get into a place where her engine can get warmed up.

Her Breasts

The breasts are a place that most men long to get back to. Call it a long-lost connection from his days of breast feeding. Every man can't wait to get back to those nectars of nature! A husband should be gentle when touching his wife's breasts. He should approach these gingerly.

Dr. Ian Kerner, author of *She Comes First*, says: "The mistake that most men make is forgetting slow equals intense. The fix: Use your thumb and index finger to gently massage her breast, first clockwise and then counterclockwise and then counterclockwise. Then place your hand over her areola, and roll it with your palm. Finally (very) gently pull and tease her nipple. Do one at a time, in slow motion. The gain. This careful, intense formula combines several kinds of stimulation, ensuring that she enjoys the experience."[3]

Her Stomach

This is a ticklish place that, if approached the right way, is also that place of extreme satisfaction. With light kisses, the velvet touch of the tongue, and the grazing of the finger tips, touching a woman's stomach can heighten the ecstasy of oral sex. Right below the belly button and above the pelvic bone is the G-spot. Pressing gently on that area from the outside of her stomach during the heightened phase of oral sex can help her to reach orgasm.

Her Inner Thighs

This is a place with multiple nerve endings. (Notice I skipped over the vagina because I am trying to show men how to start slow.) The man should take his fingertips and make figure-8s on her thighs, going up toward the vagina and then turning away right as he is getting ready to touch the vagina. The man should keep touching around the vagina until the woman writhes with pleasure, begging the man to touch her vagina.

The Back of Her Knees

The back of the knee is also a sensitive place that begs to be touched. In this area you can either use your hand, a feather, or your tongue. The idea is to touch softly to stimulate the sensitive nerves in this area. The soft caress will cause your wife to beg for you to come up a little higher. It builds the anticipation that eventually you will come up towards the vagina—but take your time, don't rush. You want to build the anticipation so that she will grab you by the ears and pull you toward her. Every woman wants to be touched like it is the first time.

Her Feet

A woman's feet need the special attention of a man. Women are on their feet so much. They pay a price to walk around in those high heels, trying to be attractive for their men. The most romantic and sensual thing a man can do is to give his woman a good foot massage. Some women like for men to suck their toes. Before diving in, a man needs to ask his wife if this is something she prefers.

Her Buttocks

The mass of muscles that compose a woman's rear end beg to be touched. Often a man wants to spank his woman in the height of passion, but this area first needs to be caressed. When the endorphins kick in after being aroused, some women may like light spanking. When a wife asks her husband to tap her bottom, he should be sure to start off light and wait for her signal as to how hard to spank. After tapping her buttocks, he should rub it in a circular motion. Sometimes a woman may like for her man to squeeze her buttocks as he is penetrating. But this is something the wife must let you know whether or not she wants.

Her Vagina Opening

Here is a place with many touch points for a man to explore. The outer lips of the vagina, the *labia majora*, have many nerve endings but are often ignored for their partners inner lips, or *labia minora*.

The clitoris is the pearl inside this shell. There is a hood over the clitoris that protects this ultra-sensitive treasure. In order for a man to get this pearl he must work with the shell. He can't pry the shell open; rather, he should love on the shell until the pearl comes out to see all of this wonderful activity taking place on the outside. There are different ways to stimulate the vagina.

The hand and fingers are able to caress the outer and inner lips. A man should make sure his hands are clean and his nails well-manicured. He can massage the lips using a safe lubricant. I don't recommend oil-based lubricants because you may forget that the oil is on your hands or get oil on your penis during penetration and this can set up infection. It is best to stick with safe lubricants like K-Y Jelly®.

Her G-Spot

The G-spot is an area two inches inside the front wall of the vagina, behind the pubic bone. When stimulated through the vagina, the G-spot expands or swells upon arousal. The G-spot has a different texture than the rest of the vagina. It can feel smoother or rougher than the vaginal walls. It can also feel like a spongy area, and be anywhere from the size of a pea to the size of a half-dollar coin. One way for a man to know that he has found the G-spot is when pressure on that area creates a sensation to urinate.

The G-spot is engorged when it is aroused. This relatively small area cannot be found unless the woman is already turned on. Trying to rub or caress the G-spot before a woman is totally stimulated can sometimes cause her discomfort or pain. The good news about G-spot orgasms is that women can have one before, during, or after a clitoral orgasm.

Couples can also use sex toys like vibrators or butterflies that stimulate the clitoris. Some Christian women may have a problem with using vibrators that are life-like because they fear that they are crossing the line of fantasizing about another man. The apostle Paul helped us with this when he said that if you think it is a sin to eat meat sacrificed to idols than you ought to avoid it. Until a woman can reconcile that the stimulation of a sex toy has nothing to do with her desiring to be with another man, then she may need to avoid toys.

Toys are tools to help bring the wife to satisfaction, and it is a turn-on for a man to see his wife turned on. When a woman knows that her husband is using toys for her benefit and not his own, she is more apt to be open to their use. For those who don't have any mental reservations, sex toys are an added tool to help the husband work on his wife's engine. They also help to save the man's tongue and hand from cramps because it takes a woman twenty to thirty minutes to reach an orgasm.

I've asked Christian women, "Why don't women just open up and tell their husbands what they really want in the bedroom?" Their answers are enlightening. Most are afraid that their husbands might assume that their inquisitiveness or their direct requests would label them as "freaks." They explained, "We have heard men talk about how Suzy Slut was a freak and did this and that, and we don't want to be considered freaks." Most men will not tell their wives that every man wants a freak, but marries a good girl. Then the married good girl is trapped with her secret sexual desires because she doesn't want her husband to think she is a "bad girl."

There is so much to the woman to explore. Once a man learns how to appreciate the complexity of the female anatomy and her emotional makeup, he will enjoy the classic gift that God has given him. Once a man learns how to start his wife's engine the way she likes for it to be started, then both will enjoy the drive that God has given them.

One pastor's wife said that she thought it would be dangerous to share her fantasies if it involved being with someone else. I agreed, but assured her that fantasies don't always have to be about being with someone other than one's spouse. But even with that, there ought to be a space where spouses share personal fantasies, understanding that means it will be put into action. It is important to create a space where couples can at least talk about it. It takes time and trust for couples to get to the point where they can be completely honest at this level.

Men and women ought to be able to ask for what they want, within the boundaries of holy matrimony, without being scorned. The Imago Dialogue helps couples explore their desires and fantasies without being judged. The Imago Dialogue is really a tool to get couples who haven't been able to say things like, "I've always wanted you to give me oral sex." Then the other spouse uses the Imago Dialogue to say, "So, what I hear you saying is that you would like me to perform oral sex on you. Is that all?" Sharing the fantasy or desire does not mean that the other spouse has to honor the request, it just means that spouse listens without judging.

There is a whole new world of sexual intimacy and enjoyment to explore once we return to the place where we are naked and have no shame. God created us to be sexual creatures. He gave us nerve endings in special places to be enjoyed by our spouses in the holy institution of marriage. What God has made clean, let no one call unclean. There is no need to be ashamed.

When a man or woman finds the soulmate that God has fashioned for him or her, it is both their obligation to fulfill each other sexually. How many marriages would have been saved if Christian couples knew how to please one another sexually and to ask for the sex they want?

Conclusion

Sex is a gift from God that is to be enjoyed. That is why we learn from Proverbs 5:18-19 (NIV), "May your fountain be blessed, and may you rejoice in the wife of your youth. A loving doe, a graceful deer (impala smile)—may her breasts satisfy you always, may you ever be captivated by her love."

This is a new day for married couples. With all of the information and inspiration available, there is no reason why Christian couples can't return to the Secret Garden and explore all that God has created, with the exception of that one tree, have fun, be naked, and don't be ashamed about anything that God has given His children to enjoy!

*The kind of romance
that fueled the courtship
is an integral part of keeping
a strong marriage.
For forty days, couples should
make it their business
to reintroduce romance
into their marriage.*

EPILOGUE
40 Days of Great Sex

Great sex starts long before a couple enters the bedroom. No one likes to be taken for granted, but when couples are married, they can quickly begin to take each other for granted, especially after they have increased responsibilities, like raising children. When a couple first meets, they are excited. They want to be near each other all the time. They stay up all night talking on the phone. They think about each other all day when they are apart. They go out on dates and relish their conversations.

The kind of romance that fueled the courtship is an integral part of keeping a strong marriage. For forty days, couples should make it their business to reintroduce romance into their marriage. They should go out on a date every week and treat the date like the most important appointment there is. They should not let anything or anybody stop them from going on this date. If they have children, investing in a baby sitter is money well spent so they can reconnect. This is especially important for women. Women need to connect emotionally before they can connect sexually.

Romance doesn't have to be expensive. A couple can have regular romantic dates that are free or relatively inexpensive.

Here are some inexpensive things that either spouse can do:

- Go for a walk
- Go to a concert in the park
- Have a picnic lunch
- Write a love letter
- Take a bath together
- Hold each other while you watch television
- Have pillow talk every night before going to sleep
- Treat each other to lunch
- A husband or wife can send flowers to the other spouse.
- Have his or her favorite food ready when coming home from work
- Download his or her favorite music on his/her iPod®.
- A wife can make a "pin-up" calendar for her husband
- A husband can wash his wife's car without her asking
- A husband can wash the dishes for his wife
- A husband and wife can worship together
- A husband and wife can pray together
- A husband and wife can renew their vows, publicly or privately
- Spouses can leave love notes for each other around the house

For the next forty days, every couple can rediscover the ecstasy of being naked and unashamed. Look at the calendar included for couples to follow (p. 165) to determine how to give each other pleasure for forty days.

	SUNDAY	MONDAY	TUESDAY	WEDNESDAY	THURSDAY	FRIDAY	SATURDAY
WEEK 1	Worship together.	Share a fantasy you want to act out, but one that does not violate your marriage covenant.	Write a seductive love letter and leave it in your spouse's underwear drawer.	Read the "Theology of Great Sex" chapter.	Have devotional time together. Read Song of Solomon 1.	Complete exercise "Getting the Sex You Want" (pp. 19-20)	Take a candlelight bath or shower together, if possible.
WEEK 2	Worship together.	Give your wife a foot massage.	Give your spouse a sensual massage at bedtime with a strong finish.	Learn more about the "Imago Dialogue" technique.	Devotional reading: Song of Solomon 4. Ask: What do you like about my body?	Go on a romantic date. Come home and do Exercise 2 (pp. 66-67).	Go shopping. Buy your wife or husband something sexy. Come home & model.
WEEK 3	Worship together.	Give your wife a full body massage with sweet-smelling oil.	Do a "quickie" in any room besides the bedroom.	Read about new ways to please your partner sexually.	Read 1 Corinthians 7. Ask: How can I please you more?	Do Exercise 3 in Getting the Sex You Want (pp. 31-33).	Unplug the TV and "turn me on!" Husbands, cook dinner or order take out.
WEEK 4	Worship together.	Spend a night of emotional sex. Hold each other naked & unashamed. Concentrate on breathing the same rhythm & maintaining eye contact for 15 minutes.	Schedule a lunch date.	Practice talking "dirty" to your spouse.	Morning: Have a romantic phone call with your spouse at a random time. Evening: Devotion: Acts 10:9. What are some things that you use to think were forbidden?	Get a hotel room and spend the night or get a baby sitter so you can have the whole house to yourselves. Do Exercise 4 (pp. 36-38).	Serve your spouse breakfast in bed.

REFERENCES & NOTES

END NOTES

Introduction

1 http://www.barna.org/FlexPage.aspx?Page=BarnaUpdate&BarnaUpdat eID=170.

Chapter One

1 Frederick Buechner, *Godric: A Novel* (New York: Harper San Francisco, 1983)

2 Leland Ryken and J. I. Packer, *Worldly Saints: The Puritans as They Really Were* (Grand Rapids: Zondervan, 1990).

3 http://www.rockart.wits.ac.za/origins/external_pages/publications/files/ Lewis-Williams%201976.%20%20Myth%20and%20message%20in%2 0Bushman%20Art.pdf.

4 Squire Rushnell and Louise DuArt, *Couples Who Pray The Most Intimate Act Between a Man and a Woman* (Nashville: Thomas Nelson, 2008)

5 Jerry W. Ward, Jr. "Dreamwork/Eros" Sections. *Dark Eros: Black Erotic Writings*, edited and annotated by Reginald Martin, Ph.D., 1997, St. Martin's Press.

6 Arterburn, Stephen, Fred Stoeker, and Mike Yorkey. *Every Man's Battle: Winning the War on Sexual Temptation One Victory at a Time.* New York: Struik, 2002.

Chapter Two

1 Martin.

Chapter Three

1 John Gray, *Why Mars and Venus Collide: Improving Relationships by Understanding How Men and Women Cope Differently with Stress* (New York: HarperCollins, 2008).

Chapter Four

1 James Hollis, *Why Good People Do Bad Things: Understanding Our Darker Selves* (New York: Gotham, 2007)

2 John Milton, *Paradise Lost* (PD)

3 Tammy Nelson, *Getting the Sex You Want: Shed Your Inhibitions and Reach New Heights of Passion Together* (Minneapolis: Quiver, 2008).

4 Nelson. p. 63.

5 http://www.cvclv.org/stats.html.

Chapter Seven

1 Robert Lewis, Shaunti Feldhahn, and Jeremy Howard, *The New Eve: Choosing God's Best for Your Life* (New York: B&H Books, 2008).

2 John Gray, *Mars and Venus in the Bedroom*: A Guide to Lasting Romance and Passion (New York: HarperCollins, 2001.

Chapter Eight

1 Sharon Ethridge, *Every Young Woman's Battle: Guarding Your Mind, Heart, and Body in a Sex-Saturated World*, (Colorado Springs, Colorado: WaterBrook Press, 2003).

Chapter Nine

1 Marsha Normandy, Joseph St. James, and Arlene Schunk, *The Handjob Handbook: A Work of Non-Friction* (New York: Simon Spotlight Entertainment, 2008).

2 "Soft First, Then Hard," *Men's Health: 20th Anniversary Collector's Edition* November 2008. p. 62.

3 Ian Kerner, *She Comes First: The Thinking Man's Guide to Pleasuring a Woman* (London: Souvenir Press, 2005).

BIBLIOGRAPHY

Arterburn, Stephen, Fred Stoeker, and Mike Yorkey. *Every Man's Battle: Winning the War on Sexual Temptation One Victory at a Time.* New York: Struik, 1920.

Bloomfield, Harold H., and Robert K. Cooper. *Power of Five: Hundreds of 5-Second to 5-Minute Scientific Shortcuts to Ignite Your Energy, Burn Fat, Stop Aging and Revitalize Your Love Life.* New York: Rodale P, Incorporated, 1997.

Buechner, Frederick. *Godric: A Novel.* New York: Harper San Francisco, 1983.

Chapman, Gary. *The Five Love Languages: How to Express Heartfelt Commitment to Your Mate.* Grand Rapids: Northfield, 1992.

Cox, Tracey. *Superhotsex.* New York: DK ADULT, 2006.

Cox, Tracey. *Supersex.* Grand Rapids: Dorling Kindersley, Incorporated, 2002.

Ethridge, Sharon. *Every Young Woman's Battle: Guarding Your Mind, Heart, and Body in a Sex-Saturated World.* Colorado Springs, Co.: WaterBrook Press, 2003.

Godson, Suzi, Peter Stemmler, and Robert Winston. *Sexploration: An Edgy Encyclopedia of Everything Sexual.* New York: Ulysses P, 2005.

Gray, John. *Mars and Venus in the Bedroom: A Guide to Lasting Romance and Passion.* New York: HarperCollins, 2001.

Gray, John. *Why Mars and Venus Collide: Improving Relationships by Understanding How Men and Women Cope Differently with Stress.* New York: HarperCollins, 2008.

Harford, Tim. *The Logic of Life : Uncovering the New Economics of Everything.* New York: Little, Brown Book Group Limited, 2008.

Harley, Willard F. *His Needs, Her Needs: Building an Affair-Proof Marriage.* New York: Baker Group, 2001.

Hollis, James. *Why Good People Do Bad Things: Understanding Our Darker Selves.* New York: Gotham, 2007.

Hutcherson, Hilda. *What Your Mother Never Told You about Sex.* New York: Tarcher, 2004.

Kerner Ian, *She Comes First: The Thinking Man's Guide to Pleasuring a Woman.* London: Souvenir Press, 2005.

Lewis, C. S. *The Four Loves.* Grand Rapids: Zondervan, 2002.

Lewis, Robert, Shaunti Feldhahn, and Jeremy Howard. *The New Eve: Choosing God's Best for Your Life.* New York: B&H Books, 2008.

Martin, Reginald, and Lenard D. Moore. "Dreamwork/Eros." *Dark Eros: Black Erotic Writings.* Ed. Reginald Martin. Boston: Saint Martin's Griffin, 1999.

Michaels, Marcy, and Marie De Salle. *Blow Him Away: How to Give Him Mind-Blowing Oral Sex.* New York: Broadway, 2004.

Michaels, Marcy, and Marie De Salle. *The Low Down on Going Down: How to Give Her Mind-Blowing Oral Sex.* New York: Broadway, 2004.

Milton, John. *Paradise Lost.* PD

Nelson, Tammy. *Getting the Sex You Want: Shed Your Inhibitions and Reach New Heights of Passion Together.* Minneapolis: Quiver, 2008.

Normandy, Marsha, Joseph St. James, and Arlene Schunk. *The Handjob Handbook: A Work of Non-Friction.* New York: Simon Spotlight Entertainment, 2008.

Rushnell, Squire, and Louise DuArt. *Couples Who Pray: The Most Intimate Act Between a Man and a Woman.* Nashville: Thomas Nelson, 2008.

Ryken, Leland, and J. I. Packer. *Worldly Saints: The Puritans as They Really Were.* Grand Rapids: Zondervan, 1990.

"Soft First, Then Hard." Men's Health: 20th Anniversary Collector's Edition, November 2008.

Wilson, P. B. and Bunny Wilson. *Liberated Through Submission: God's Design for Freedom in All Relationships.* New York: Harvest House, 1997.

ABOUT THE AUTHOR
Stacy L. Spencer, D.Min.

*A*s pastor of the congregation ranked by Outreach Magazine (2008) as the fastest-growing church in Tennessee and nineteenth fastest-growing in U.S., Dr. Stacy L. Spencer is arguably becoming one of the country's emerging pastoral leaders and visionaries. This man of humble beginnings now serves as senior pastor of New Direction Christian Church in Memphis, Tennessee, which has grown to a membership of more than thirteen thousand members in only seven years.

The Olmstead, Kentucky, native started New Direction as a church plant of Mississippi Boulevard Christian Church in 2001, with roughly sixty members. Throughout the organization's brief history, the ministry has created numerous avenues for God's vision to manifest. In 2004, Dr. Spencer donated New Direction's original facility, including a fourteen-thousand-square-feet Sprung structure to a Hispanic congregation, Nueva Direccion. Nueva Direccion Christian Church now ministers to more than six hundred Hispanics weekly.

In March 2005, New Direction opened its second location, New Direction Collierville, to serve the emerging diverse community beyond the Memphis city limits. In 2007, New Direction expanded internationally with the launch of New Direction Christian Centre in Dutwya, South Africa.

New Direction's global ministry continues to grow with the January 2009 launch of the ministry's online radio station, PowerZoneRadio.org. This twenty-four-hour weekday format features sermons and devotions by Dr. Spencer and other notable pastors, plus contemporary gospel, gospel jazz, Christian Hip Hop, and talk shows. Dr. Spencer is a tech-savvy pastor who ministers to thousands throughout cyberspace using FaceBook.com, Twitter.com, YouTube.com, and MySpace.com. People also can connect with the ministry each Tuesday at 10 a.m. on Comcast Channel 17, and through live streams of Sunday and Tuesday worship services via N2Newdirection.org.

Dr. Spencer serves as chairman of the board of directors, for the Power Center Community Development Corporation. The independent, non-profit Power Center CDC launched in 2006 with the focus to restore the economic, educational, and social foundation of the Hickory Hill community through empowering initiatives designed to instill hope, pride, and a sense of community. In August 2008, Power Center CDC launched the Power Center Academy, a Memphis City Schools Charter School, educating more than one hundred sixth-grade students. The school focuses on high technology, financial literacy, and community service and has plans to add grades 7 and 8 over a two-year period. Through a partnership with Apple Computers, students are given laptops and are taught comprehensive online skills. In partnership with SunTrust Bank, students gain hands-on experience balancing their finances and entrepreneurship through SunTrust's only on-site student branch.

Dr. Spencer also serves as an officer of Power Center Enterprises, parent company of Soul Café restaurant and Fillin' Station and Fillin' Station II Bookstores. Soul Café is the first of its kind in Memphis, offering an upscale yet casual dining experience in an eclectic setting with wireless high-speed Internet connections and live Christian entertainment. Soul Café has more than twenty employees. The eatery is the site of Dr. Spencer's popular Power

Lunch series held Wednesdays at noon. He teaches marketplace leaders inspirational business and life principles to take their spiritual, business, and personal skills to the next level. Power Lunch is streamed live via stacyspencer.org and features an online chat where viewers can pose questions to and interact with Dr. Spencer. Fillin' Station Bookstores offer the latest in Bibles, contemporary Christian best-sellers, reference resources, inspirational novelty items, apparel, and Dr. Spencer's sermons.

Because he is passionate about building positive economic enterprises in urban communities, he has invested his personal resources to launch a new business venture—Wash & Cuts, a full-service, upscale barber, beauty, and car care salon in the heart of the Hickory Hill community. Beyond bringing a positive business to the community, Spencer plans for the business to give back even more with the Gifted Hands program, an apprentice program to help young people learn relevant employment skills.

Dr. Spencer launched 2009 with the release of Naked and Unashamed, a resource that is aimed at helping Christian married couples begin the journey toward sexual fulfillment. The impetus for the book was his widely successful Bible study, "40 Nights of Great Sex." More than four hundred diverse couples attended the five-week marriage seminar. The interactive classes, co-facilitated by his wife, Rhonda F. Spencer, were profiled in *Time* magazine and garnered international attention from France and Germany.

He and Rhonda are the proud parents of four sons: Calvin, Omari, Jordan, and Jaden Lynn.

Education

- Doctor of Ministry, Drew University, Madison, N.J. (1999)
- Master of Divinity, Southern Baptist Theological Seminary, Louisville, Ky. (1993)
- Bachelor of Arts, Broadcast Communication, Western Kentucky University, Bowling Green, Ky. (1990)

Community Involvement

- 2001 — Recognized as a "Top Gun under 40 in Memphis" by the *Black Business Directory*
- 2003–Present — Board of Directors, National Civil Rights Museum in Memphis
- 2005 — Named one of Memphis' "Top 40 under 40" by the *Memphis Business Journal*
- 2005 — Chairperson, Lifeblood's Hope 4 Healing Campaign
- 2005 — Pastor of the Year, Memphis Gospel Bridge Awards
- 2005 — Selected among 60 pastors in the Tri-State area for the Sustained Pastoral Excellence (SPE) program
- Member, Kappa Alpha Psi Fraternity, Incorporated

Published Works

- 2001 — sermon featured in the "Top 20 Pastors under 40" edition of *The African American Pulpit*, Judson Press.
- 2001 — "Little People Can Do Big Things Too," a sermon featured in *The African American Pulpit*. This sermon is personally close as the Spencer's son, Jordan, has Achondroplasia.
- 2007 — daily devotional featured in 365 Meditations for Men by Men, Abingdon Press
- 2009 — published *Naked and Unashamed: The Journey Toward Sexual Fulfillment in Christian Marriage*.

• • • • • •

If you are interested in inviting Dr. Spencer to speak at an upcoming event, or would like to host a "40 Days of Great Sex" workshop, please contact Lori McGee, executive assistant, by phone at 877.686.6322 or via e-mail at mcgee.lori@stacyspencer.org.

To learn more about New Direction Christian Church, Dr. Spencer, or any of the aforementioned initiatives, visit www.n2newdirection.org, www.stacyspencer.org, soulcafememphis.com, powerzoneradio.org, powercentercdc.org or washandcuts.com.

Printed in the United States
152421LV00003B/2/P

9 780981 971018